HEART FOR THE GAME

by
SIMON KEITH
with
JASON COLE
and
DON YAEGER

Nexus Publishing, Inc.

ISBN: 978-1475195132

DEDICATION

To the brave families who, in their darkest hour, had the courage to unselfishly give the ultimate gift of life to others.

"Out of Tragedy comes Hope"

CONTENTS

FOREWORD

BY STEVE NASH

I come from the same place as Simon Keith, literally and figuratively.

From growing up in Victoria, British Columbia, to attending the same high school for a time, Simon and I share so much. We're undersized and were overlooked. Like Simon, soccer has been a passion of mine since I was born (even if I ended up in the NBA). We're the sons of immigrant English and Welsh parents. We are Canadian. We are athletes.

Once you get past some of those facts, Simon's path to the professional ranks represents a journey with odds much steeper than mine - a self described, slow, white, Canadian point guard, with exactly one scholarship offer.

All athletes have their own personal challenges as they rise through the ranks of their sport. Simon's were unique. I try and imagine a doctor telling me at age 20 that I had six weeks to live, that my heart was about to give out on me. I envision me and my family having to travel 5,000 miles to finally get the heart that was so desperately needed just as time was about to run out. What Simon was facing at that point in his career would stop most kids in their tracks. But I understand where Simon comes from.

I understand that our shared upbringings allowed us to dream. So Simon decided to take it a step further. A lot of steps further. Long strides, actually. With a pacemaker bulging from his chest, Simon continued to chase the goal to actually *play* again. Not in a rec league and not just in college.

As a professional.

I have spent my professional career playing against some of the greatest athletes in the world. Each train hard, have a burning desire for their sport and have inevitably overcome some kind of adversity. I have never met an athlete who overcame Simon's circumstances. To say the odds of playing soccer again were overwhelming doesn't even begin to explain what he did.

Just living required overcoming long odds. To live for more than 25 years makes Simon one of the longest-living heart transplant recipients in the world. To put that in perspective, the average life expectancy at the time he had the surgery was less than seven years. Put it all together and you have a physical achievement that is truly unparalleled.

All these years later, Simon has gone on a pilgrimage to help readers understand his journey. That pilgrimage includes a dramatic meeting with the father of the young man who died and whose heart was donated to Simon. Their meeting, 25 years after that fateful day when the father lost his son and Simon gained a life, takes place in the perfect setting. The soccer field where the young man had ironically died while playing soccer, looks like any number of fields that bring back memories of our youth. A soccer field for us represents our childhood, and the uninhibited natural passion we have for the game. For Simon this field represented life.

I encourage people to read the story of how Simon became the first person to ever come back from a heart transplant to play professional sports. Making his return was beyond guts and determination.

Obviously, much of that courage comes from his parents, a Welsh father and an English mother who left the mother country in the 1960s, just like my folks did at roughly the same time. Our parents came to Canada to escape economic hardship and make a better life for us. Ironically, both our sets of parents made a brief stop in Saskatchewan before continuing west and settling in Victoria. They were selfless, tough-minded people.

Both our fathers passed an infectious passion for soccer to us. We both played the beautiful game practically from the time we could walk, going through Victoria's great youth program. For Simon, two older brothers helped push him to greater and greater levels, key to cementing his love for the game. For me, it was a younger brother and younger sister who provided the natural opponents growing up.

As a fellow athlete, I completely identify with the will sports creates in those of us who give ourselves to the game. For each of us, Victoria was the backdrop for this passion. There was a culture of amateur sports that made healthy competition part of our DNA and made dreams of athletic success possible.

In this book, Simon takes you through all of that, from the building blocks his parents provided to make him strong, to the environment in Victoria that provided everything he needed to succeed. That includes a community that supported him and his family in a time of need. The expression that it takes a village to raise a child couldn't be more appropriate than in this story. The great people of Victoria mobilized to raise money to cover the huge expenses that weren't covered by Canada's healthcare program.

With a great community support system in place, coupled with a passion for sports imprinted by our shared youth, Simon attempted something so far beyond people's imagination that even his closest family and friends were anxious. But belief and desire are strong partners.

Like any great athlete who is told he can't do something, Simon took that talk and turned it into fuel for his desire. As a result, Simon chose a path that I associate very clearly with. Chasing his goals in the United States (through college and later professional soccer) allowed Simon the opportunity to follow his dreams. What he achieved is simply extraordinary.

This is a story about the human spirit. It will inspire. It will motivate. It will make you laugh and it will make you cry. It is a story of hope and determination. It is an incredible saga. It is a story of almost unbelievable luck coupled with world class perseverance. And after all that it is still so much more.

1

A Welsh Heart

I stand to the right of a gentle, 71-year-old man, staring at the grave of the 17-year-old son he lost 25 years ago. To his left stand my teenage son and daughter arm-in-arm, comforting one another. As the elderly man begins to cry, feeling guilty over his son's tragically imperfect body, I am uncomfortably thankful for the flaw.

Because his son's heart still beats in my body.

To be clear, this wonderful man I'm standing with is happy for me and thankful that the parts of his son that were donated didn't go to waste. Robert Fields -- I've changed his name to protect his family from unwanted attention -- is warm, generous, funny, comforting and extremely intelligent. He's that story-telling grandfather from a Hallmark Channel movie and this couldn't have been a more perfect meeting. But, at this moment, after we tour the Welsh city where his son grew up, died and is buried, the moment is raw and the sadness comes rushing back.

Robert breaks down in tears. His son, James, was an innocent 17-year-old when an aneurysm ruptured in his head, filling the area around his brain with blood and causing him to die shortly thereafter. He was bright, industrious, clever and cheerful, a model son and so greatly loved that at least one of his friends named his first child after him. These many years later, James' mother hurts deeply. So do his older brother and sister. In so many ways, James was a perfect child, except for the one imperfection that Robert still blames himself for.

Robert gathers himself and lightly jokes that he's "a big softie." I tell the writer I've hired to do this book to let him be. "We've done enough to him today," I say. We have been at this for hours and, by now, I'm a jumble of emotions myself: Thankful, solemn, overjoyed, reflective, surprised, curious and energized. A million thoughts flow through me as I try to figure out what to say, how to say it and even when to say it.

Fields walks away with my kids, and I hold a silent conversation with his departed son. I tell him, "we're gonna do this. This may be more complex and complicated than I ever imagined, but we're gonna get this done."

It has taken me a long time to get to this point, literally and figuratively. Now that I have reached it, as I take it all in, I begin to realize the full enormity of everything that has happened to bring me here. I have spent the better part of the day with this wonderful man, learning about his son and his family, and it has all become overwhelming. So much so, that my children joke intermittently, "What happened to you?"

Normally, I can't stop talking. I'm a chatterbox, a jokester, a lecturer, a slightly hyperactive man with an opinion on just about everything. But today is different. Today, I'm taking it all in, getting a really big picture about how this has all really worked. Up to a certain point, you can understand how so many people come into your life over the years, and how they help shape who you are. You can use whichever cliché you prefer -- how it takes a village or how no one does it alone. That's all true. But it my extreme case, this is a mystery that's almost impossible to explain.

Back in my hometown of Victoria, Canada, I have two wonderful parents. They didn't just raise me. Their pioneer spirit rubbed off on me. They gave me courage and a strong, sometimes stubborn will. I have my two older brothers, and a list of hundreds and hundreds of other family members and friends between Canada and England who all took part in saving my life. I had financial benefactors and a laundry list of doctors who helped. One of those doctors risked his career in order to fight the politics of heart transplants in England, paving the way for people like me to live. He was so noble in his battle that he has been knighted by Queen Elizabeth II. We're not talking just about villages that helped raise me and kept me alive, we're talking about nations. We're not just talking about everyday people who opened their hearts to help me. We're also talking about historical figures in the field of medicine. We're also talking about family. Not just my family. We're talking about how much another family lost, in order to give me a second chance at life.

Overwhelmed would be an understatement.

For most of the 25 years before this moment, I have lived with blinders on. The blinders you need to be an athlete, a competitor and a survivor. I have done all three with my second chance. Not only was I the first heart transplant patient to ever play professional sports (golfer Erik Compton is the only other), I have also become one of the world's longest-living heart transplant recipients. Most heart transplant recipients are lucky to make it 10 years. On top of that, I got married, had a family and made money in the high-pressure world of Las Vegas entertainment. After all this, I finally reached a point of reflection. I finally wanted to know what happened to make it all possible.

I am, as the writer Malcolm Gladwell, described so well in his profound work on successful people, an Outlier. "Outliers" achieve vastly different kinds of success or fortune and some are absurdly famous, like the Beatles or Bill Gates. I haven't created great music or been at the forefront of changing the way the world does business. What I did was simply survive and thrive. What I did was live life to the fullest I knew how. Like most of those outliers, I had certain advantages. I was conditioned by sports and given a body that could recover from the trauma of losing one heart and accepting another. I had a simple, straightforward approach to life. I had people around me who supported me.

And I had just enough luck and fortunate circumstance. I had dual citizenship between Canada and England. I was born at the right time to take advantage of advances in transplant surgery, both technologically and politically. I was at the right time and right place to get the perfect heart to fit my body. Finally, I had the great fortune to be given a gift from James and his parents. I was the ultimate beneficiary of their generosity.

Now, all these years later, I wanted to know whose heart beat in my body. I knew some cursory details about how James had died, but not enough. I wanted to know what he was like – any and every detail. What did he do?

What did he study? Did he have a girlfriend? Most of all, I just wanted to say thank you to the family that lost so much and gave me everything.

So here I am back in Wales standing in a cemetery next to a man who I can't thank enough and, for the first time in my life, feeling introspective. Part of this is truly uncomfortable, an uneasy place I have never allowed myself to go. As I talked to Robert earlier in the day, I couldn't help but repeat to myself again and again.

How do you say thank you to someone who gave you … everything?

For me, the answer has always been to live a full and complete life. Up to this point, I viewed my heart transplant in a seemingly callous way. "One out, one in" is how I used to describe the procedure, as if you were changing the battery in a flashlight or fixing a tire. A lot of people I know who have been through a transplant procedure can't let go of the fear they lived with before the operation. Their identity becomes that of a transplant patient, as if they are some piece of delicate china. And trust me, when I say that the attitude doesn't come from just the people themselves, it comes from all around you. When you have a transplant, people view you in a different way. Family, friends, even passing strangers who might know a smidgen of your story, treat you as if your life should be handled with kid gloves. It's like you should have "Fragile: Handle With Care" stamped across your forehead.

Our culture contributes to that idea. There are all these movies about transplants. Literally, you can find hundreds of movies in all sorts of genres about transplants. There are romantic comedies (*Return to Me*), horror flicks (start with *Frankenstein* in 1931 and continue right up to 2010 with *Repo Men*) and a vast assortment of titles that emphasize the mystic quality, particularly with heart transplants, such as *Tell Tale*, *A Stranger's Heart* and *All About Love*.

I'm the opposite of all that. I talk about my transplant in the most matter-of-fact way. Even Robert tried to downplay the mysticism of it. He spoke of a conversation he had with his family doctor before he came to meet me. His doctor tried to ease the situation by saying, "Really, when you think about it, it's just a pump." I've viewed my transplant much the same way. I did it intentionally because it was the only way to persuade people that I was OK. I got plenty of stares, but I never flinched. I never let on about how close to death I had really been. I never let anyone in on the emotions because, well, I didn't let myself in on them, either. This is how it works for athletes. You don't look back. You look forward. If you get hurt, you get better and you get back on the field. It's that simple. If you want to be great at something, there's not a lot of room for introspection. The people competing against you certainly don't care if you're hurt. So you better not worry about how you feel.

Conversely, as I walked across the soccer field where Robert's son James had died 25 years earlier, it's as if my calloused psyche has been filed completely smooth. It's not just the deep coincidences like we both played soccer or that my own father was born less than 20 miles from this exact field. Try being callous to pain as you imagine James' mother, Paula, running onto this field and finding her son dying. Try ignoring the simple reality that if none of that ever happened, my children and I wouldn't be here today. All the emotions I have spent a lifetime avoiding are churning through me. On this field right now, I find myself at a place and moment in time that I have tried to block from my mind forever.

And yet, now, more than anything, I want to understand and feel it all.

Earlier in the day, when we first met Robert Fields, he brought pictures of James, who had red hair and freckles. My son, Sean, has red hair and freckles, even though there aren't any other red heads we know of on either side of our large extended family. All of a sudden, I was wondering if Sean got his hair color from James. Sean and James have the same middle name – Edward. Sean and James even look a little bit alike.

Like my parents, James' parents traveled the world. James was born in the United States and went to England; I was born in England and ended up in the United States. My father was a physical education teacher and coach. James' mother was a P.E. teacher and coach. James was a budding entrepreneur who once paid his father to buy some teen-fashion shirts on a trip to Hong Kong, intending to then turn a profit. Part of my business when I got started in Las Vegas was selling t-shirts at casinos and shows that I imported from Hong Kong.

I started to wonder if this was something more mystical than just finding the perfect pump for my body. Did I not just find someone whose physical size and blood type matched me well enough for a snug fit, but also someone who was a kindred spirit? Have I not just spent my life living out my dreams, but maybe some of his as well?

It's all really fascinating to wonder about as I walk with my daughter Sam on this field where my life was essentially saved as another one was taken. In a sense, this is where my life begins, at least my second chance at life. Before James Fields died unexpectedly, I was lying in bed a couple of hours away, dying a little more each minute as my heart degenerated. By then, I had been sick for almost two years. I had been turned down for a transplant in Canada and had come to England in desperation. I had spent weeks in my relatives' home and eventually in a hospital, worrying, hoping and praying. I was bedridden, growing increasingly pale with each passing day as my mother and father watched helplessly. It's a hell of a thing to wait for someone to die so that you might live. But that's what this situation came down to in its most basic form. When you think about it in those terms, you also realize you better not waste the gift when you receive it.

I don't just mean the gift that James gave me. There was all the hard work of my parents. The generosity of the people back home in Victoria. There was the pushy work of Sir Terence English, the doctor who not only approved me for my transplant, but the man who wouldn't let those around him stop his heart transplant project in the 1970s. English went from being derided as a man who "dealt in death" to receiving the highest honor in English culture, knighthood. There was Dr. Mohsin Hakim, who told me simply that the goal of having heart transplant surgery was to return to the life I had before. He was the same man who helped my wife Kelly time after time in dealing with the pressures and concerns of having married a heart transplant recipient.

There are the teammates, the coaches and the executives in soccer who pushed me physically, helping me achieve my dream of playing again. There were the college administrators and coaches who bent the rules and took a chance on the seemingly insane idea of letting a guy with a heart transplant play soccer. If I had died playing soccer after my heart transplant, do you realize how many people could have lost their job for taking that kind of risk?

To honor all those sacrifices and gambles, I will tell you the story of what I gained. Just as important, I hope I can convey this message to anyone else out there in the transplant community. For so many transplant recipients I have met over the years, there's this tendency to treat your life as if you live in a bubble. To me, that's counterintuitive. I resisted becoming "The Heart Guy" to the people back in my hometown because I didn't want to be defined by that term. I didn't want my life to be about being a heart transplant recipient.

I have always wanted to just be a guy, a normal guy. A guy who smokes a cigar or has a beer from time to time. A guy who eats a greasy hamburger or some fries when he wants to. I wanted to live out my dreams on a soccer field. I wanted to get married and have kids. I wanted to grow old. I wanted to just live and I have done that and more.

For so many people whom I have encountered, they live more out of fear than out of fearlessness. They remember what it was like as they waited for the transplant, immersed in the fear that it might not happen in time and that they might die. And so many more people, for whatever reason, live their life out of some sense of fear; as if the goal in life is to rid the world of what you are afraid of, instead of just living without fear. I am writing this book for you too.

There are a million places I could start this story, a million significant moments I now look back at in wonder. But I choose to start it in this place, on a beautiful day in August 2011 in Wales. Standing right here, next to this gentle man who still cries over what his son lost.

2

MY BIG GAMBLE

I'm in my mid-40s as I write this book and I have spent more than half my life in Las Vegas, my second home. But my biggest gamble came long before I got here.

By March 1986, I was 20 and well into the second year of my heart degenerating because of an aggressive virus. The technical name for what I had was myocarditis, an inflammation of the heart muscle. In October 1984, when I was 19, I got sick after playing in a tournament in Regina, Canada. I remained sick for longer than normal and the symptoms got progressively worse. I would wake up feeling tired. Even after I seemed to shake the cold, I was losing strength in my body. There was something seriously wrong. My inflamed heart muscle started to become permanently damaged. Explaining it now is easy, but getting a doctor to figure out what it was at the time was another thing, and the cause of extreme frustration.

The way I initially noticed something was seriously wrong was that my hands were getting extremely cold, turning shockingly white and staying that way all the time. One day at practice on a typically cold, wet, Victoria winter day, I kept putting my hands inside my sweats every time there was a lull in the action. My coach, Bruce Twamley, known for his demanding coaching style, started screaming at me, thinking I wasn't into practicing or was being disrespectful. To be honest, I was cold because of lack of circulation, and I didn't even notice how much I was putting my hands in my sweats or covering them with the long sleeves of my shirt. I was just so cold. It was

11

almost like a subconscious or involuntary reaction. Twamley, known for his sharp tongue, accused me of having a bad attitude. Things got testy.

Eventually, Twamley suspended me for a couple of weeks. It was shortly after that incident when my mom noticed how white my hands had become. As I would find out, the condition of my heart and its ability to circulate the blood through my body were getting progressively worse.

My parents took me to our family doctor who thought I had an extended circulatory problem. He sent me to a specialist who, quite frankly, didn't know what he was talking about. Or as my dad said, "He was an idiot."

The so-called specialist looked me over and said he thought my symptoms were stress-related. Seriously? I was 19 years old, extremely fit, I loved life, and I was gearing up for a chance to play on the Canadian World Cup team, and this specialist thinks my hands are cold because of stress?

What followed was a run of doctors, examinations, biopsies, poking and prodding until it was finally discovered that I had myocarditis. Inflammation of the heart muscle that lead to decreased function.

From that point, and for months at a time, my condition fluctuated. Among other treatments, I underwent chemotherapy and got to the point where I felt "healthy" again. Things seemed to be going OK and by December '85 I got to play for the University of Victoria in an exhibition against the Canadian National team. The national team was set to play in nine days against Paraguay and had left a few open spots on its roster. I was a teenager with a very realistic chance for a spot on this historic team. Canada had never played in the World Cup. This would be our best team ever. I had a chance for a spot at history and glory, an opportunity to play on the biggest stage in the world of sports.

Talk about an intoxicating dream! It was enough to get me through that game, even on a cold and rainy night, and do well enough to get invited onto the national team by coach Tony Waiters afterwards. Sadly, the effort was also enough to put me back in the hospital. That night after the game, I could barely get up the stairs at the stadium. It was brutal, no question, and my mom, Sylvia had seen enough. She and my dad, David took me to the Vancouver General Hospital for another round of tests. By the turn of the year into 1986, my condition had gotten worse again. It was easy for people to see how much weight I had lost. How sick I had become. I couldn't train and I couldn't play.

The doctors had mentioned I might need a transplant if things didn't get better, but I remember thinking right up until the last minute that they were just talking the talk. The doctors were just laying out the worst-case scenario, but it wasn't a real possibility. In my mind, I always thought that being sick was purely a temporary situation. It's sort of like how doctors tell you when you get a small mole of skin cancer and you think the worst for a day or two. Then logic takes over and you get the mole burned off and all is well. I just thought, logically, that I was going to get my heart fixed the same way. To that point, I had been on chemotherapy treatments of prednisone and cyclophosphamide. I figured that the doctors would eventually find the right drug or combination of drugs and I would get better.

I felt exactly that way right up to March 3, 1986.

That day, I was sitting in a wheelchair in Vancouver General Hospital waiting to meet with Dr. Donald Ricci, an expert cardiologist who had trained with heart surgery pioneer Dr. Norman Shumway at Stanford University. I was thinking how insulting it was to be in a wheelchair when I should be up walking around on my own. By this time, I had lost a significant amount of weight and couldn't play soccer because my stamina had declined. Coming to Ricci's office at Vancouver General had become an annoying routine, including the hour-and-45-minute ferry ride from Victoria, and the usual array of pokes and prods that went with every doctor visit.

So there I was, sitting in the wheelchair in the waiting room, getting impatient as my father talked to Ricci in his office. I felt like I was waiting for the judge to deliberate my sentence. My dad – acting as my attorney –was pleading my case, but ultimately Dr. Ricci would act as judge and jury.

Ricci called me into his office and delivered his verdict:

"You have six months to live."

He continued:

"You need a heart transplant right now, and we need to do it within 10 days."

That's how I remember it because that's how I translated it – direct and to the point. I'm sure Dr. Ricci's manner was more compassionate, but I boiled it down in my head to the basic facts. It was the harshest sentence I could ever imagine coming out of another person's mouth, even though the doctors had warned me that this could happen.

My father and I tried to focus, but I was completely devastated at this moment. An indescribable, sickening feeling that seemed to drain every ounce of energy out of body. For the next few hours, I felt like I was moving outside of my body. Everything was moving in slow motion. It felt like my body wasn't actually doing anything. I know that I ended up at my brother Marc's apartment in Vancouver, but I can't remember how I got there.

I didn't say anything of any substance for a few hours. I don't know if I talked at all. For the very first time the illness, that I had now battled for almost 2 years, had gotten the better of me. For an instant it had won. But only for an instant. After the news started to sink in, my brain switched back. Back to me. The athlete started to rise up. I started to think about the practical realities. I had just taken a pretty big punch to the gut, figuratively, and it took awhile to get my brain around it.

Where did I have to go? What's the first step? When can I get it? Even then, there were things I didn't understand, like what was this going to cost? How could we pay for it? When you're 20 years old, how do you fathom what the price of a heart transplant will be? It's such a foreign concept when you're that age. I was thinking about how soon I could get back to playing soccer and whether I still had a chance to play in the World Cup that summer. That's how lightly I had taken this idea of a transplant up to this moment. I had no idea of the reality I was facing.

Get it fixed, move on. This is the attitude I inherited from my dad. I had to shift my focus now on having the surgery. This was how my brain was working.

My first stop in search of a new heart was at the University of Western Ontario Hospital in London, Ontario, roughly 2,500 miles from Victoria. The city sits halfway between Detroit and Toronto on the north side of Lake Erie directly opposite Cleveland. At the time, this was the closest hospital to my home in Canada that did heart transplants.

My father and I were the only ones who made this trip. My mother didn't go because we didn't have the money and, frankly, it would have been too much of a strain for all of us. My mother is the emotional person in our family. I love her dearly and I understand her, but she wears her heart on her sleeve. Her emotions come out first and then she works through it. When my dad called her with the news from Dr. Ricci, she got very upset. She's the perfect match for my father, who is so subdued and focused.

When you're in the middle of a fight like this, you need complete focus. You can't sit around and get swallowed up by what might go wrong or how things could fail. You can't take a minute to feel sorry for yourself. It's like in a game where you're not just playing against the opponent, but you're playing against a clock. There's no time for getting down about what happened during the previous minute or five minutes. You can't worry about a mistake, whether it's your own or the other team or the ref or whatever. You have to move on and stay focused. You don't have a choice in the matter. That's the mentality I had to keep at this point.

Particularly with what we were about to be told.

When we got to Ontario, I was taking a heavier than usual dose of prednisone. Prednisone had become not only a life-saver for me but also something like a security blanket. Prednisone is like the "wonder steroid." In 1950, a scientist named Dr. Arthur Nobile used a bacteria to oxidize cortisone into prednisone. I'm sure that's an overly simplistic explanation of what he did, but even that probably sounds too complicated for most people to understand. To that point, doctors had been using cortisone as a primary treatment for rheumatoid arthritis. By 1955, Nobile patented prednisone and prednisolone. Since then, those forms and other derivations have been used to treat asthma, COPD, ulcerative colitis, skin disorders and cerebral edema caused by cancer. We're talking about one of the great catch-all drugs of all-time. This may not be Jonas Salk curing polio, but Nobile certainly created something with a wide-ranging impact. For me it was the drug that kept me alive.

The doctors in Ontario put me through a battery of tests. My face was really bloated, but I otherwise looked healthy and was a champion on all the stress tests. I've never been on any serious stimulants, but being on prednisone has gotta be as close to that as you could imagine. I was there for a week and was as high as a kite on a windy day. I was feeling strong again, almost like I could go out and play. They put me on a treadmill. Other transplant candidates were huffing and puffing after three or four minutes. "Normal" people tapped out at 12-15 minutes.

I thought by working hard when I was in Ontario that I would prove to the doctors how deserving I was of a transplant. I wanted to show how hard I would work once I got a second chance. I was trying to do everything I could to impress them with my will and desire. So I went for it. I ran as fast as I could for 35 minutes. I didn't understand how I was actually undermining my own cause in the eyes of the doctors.

During the trip, my dad and I drove down to Detroit to see a National Hockey League game. Russ Courtnall, who grew up in Victoria, was playing for the Toronto Maple Leafs against the Detroit Red Wings. This was early in Courtnall's glorious career that spanned 17 years in the NHL after being the No. 7 overall pick in 1983.

He was also my competition at one point. Not really, except in my mind. The mind of an athlete. We played soccer together until we were 13, when he decided to focus on hockey. Russ was my age and the best hockey player in Victoria. I wanted to be the best soccer player in town so Russ provided a natural measuring stick for me and my career. Eventually, he worked his way up and became pretty much everything you dream about when you're a kid. Clearly I was on a similar path so I watched Russ's career with great interest.

When we got to Ontario, we called him up to get tickets and set up a time to meet the day of the game. We met for lunch and got caught up. All I could remember was looking at him and realizing where I was in this whole process. Here was the guy I would kind of measure myself against and he was playing his sport, making great money, and basically living the life.

Here I was, waiting for a transplant.

Don't get me wrong, Courtnall is a great guy and it was great to see him. But the fact that we were at such opposite ends of the spectrum was really tough for me to handle. I don't really let myself get depressed, but this was as down as I ever remember feeling. We went to the game at historic Joe Louis Arena and I even bought a Detroit Red Wings t-shirt that night. Still, I couldn't get the image of my circumstance out of my head.

Back in Ontario, the hospital gave me a psychological profile. It was some type of test about what I was thinking and how I was approaching this moment in my life. So here I am talking to some women I've never met before about how I feel about what's going on. Needless to say, I didn't say much on the couch. I didn't have a bunch of problems. I had one problem. That was my view. My heart was eroding as I sat there and I needed a new one.

When I didn't open up to this women the way she figured I was supposed to, they held it against me, like I was unstable or something. I was 20 and trying to fight through this mentally. I wasn't looking for someone to pour my heart out to because I didn't want to think about the problems. I wanted a solution. I wanted to fix what was wrong, not wallow in it. It's not like I had done something wrong that I should feel guilty about. I got a virus that attacked my heart. I was unlucky. I didn't abuse my body with drugs. I didn't smoke or eat so much that I destroyed my heart. I didn't have some long-term depression that led to self-destructive behavior and a heart problem. I didn't need to open up about anything. I just got sick. That was it. I had a physical problem and I needed to get it fixed. It was a simple as that to me.

The conversations would go something like this:

"Tell me a little about yourself, Simon."

"I'm a soccer player and I need a new heart so I can play again."

"Do you think a new heart will help you play again?"

"I don't know. I hope so."

"What if it doesn't?"

"I don't think about things like that."

These people in Ontario couldn't believe I viewed it that way. At one point, my dad said to me, "You've got to play the game a little bit with them if you want to get this done." But I didn't know any other way. I was being myself. I was answering their questions.

Soon after my dad gave me that advice, a psychologist asked me if I was scared. I truly wasn't scared, but I said, "Sure, I'm a little scared." I was thinking to myself, can we just get moving on this already?

Unfortunately, the answer to my question was no.

After all the tests and all the psychological profiling they did on me, the doctors in Ontario told me that I wasn't sick enough to get a heart transplant. To them, I didn't even need one. Never mind what the doctors back home were telling me. In fact, it probably worked against me that my doctors back home told me I needed a transplant. The doctors in Ontario were acting like: "No one tells US who needs a transplant. We decide who needs a transplant." Never mind that Ricci had studied under Shumway, one of the world's greatest cardiologists and the second man to ever perform a transplant. Never mind what the doctors in Ontario should have seen from the previous 18 months of examinations. My father and I were dumbfounded. In essence, what they were telling me is that all of these 40- and 50-year-old patients were going to be ahead of me in line because they looked worse than I did.

The policy at Ontario (and at a lot of places at the time) was to help the sickest person first. In other words, whoever was closest to death was first in line. I was being told: "You're not sick enough. Go home, get sicker and then come back."

I understand compassion and the desperate desire to keep someone alive. We all want to help people in need. The problem here was that heart transplants are rare and the chance for real, long-term success is complicated. Thankfully, as organ donation has become more mainstream, the medical community has also upgraded their standards for prioritizing who should get a heart transplant first. It's a complicated formula that takes into account a patient's overall health and chance for long-term success. At the time we were in Ontario, the reaction of the doctors there was really hard to accept. To my father, it felt like emotional politics.

I'm not saying I deserved a heart more than the next guy. I was simply focused on getting a transplant and getting better. To be told I was too healthy and didn't need a transplant at all -- when my doctors back home were telling me I needed to get this done in 10 days -- was extremely frustrating. After what I had been told by Ricci, it was emotionally confusing. I knew that my heart was dying. I knew I was in deep trouble. Yet for some reason the professionals in Ontario deemed that I was not a worthy candidate.

When I look back, I'm glad that I didn't have the operation in Ontario, because the whole mindset there was wrong for me. They weren't focused on getting people to move on and get healthy. They seemed to focus on the trauma and the fear and all the emotions that go with a transplant. To me, that's not feeding a positive, strong attitude. Sure, those emotions play into it, but you have to focus on how best to move forward. A transplant recipient may need to focus on life changes, new diets or giving up bad habits. But in order to live fully, you can't glorify the trauma of the past. You can't risk letting the passion necessary for recovery be dragged down by trauma and fear. I was different, and I understood this. My body was prepared to move on. Yes, a heart transplant is a traumatic thing, no question. But what's your alternative? To me, there was no value in wallowing in the situation. That's just a waste of energy. I'd rather use that energy to move forward.

When we got back to Victoria, the first thing my dad said was:

"OK, what's our next move?"

As we tried to figure that out, we had reporters to deal with. By this time in Victoria, because of my ability as a soccer player and my declining health, I had become something of a "celebrity". I had to look at it that way because I didn't like it, but the media and a lot of other people were paying attention to me. Don't get me wrong, attention is a nice thing, particularly in a wonderful, tight-knit community like Victoria.

But you want attention for the right reasons, and this didn't feel right. This is not how I wanted people to view me, as someone who needed their pity. The good thing is that people reached out to help me. As early as October 1985, people in the community started raising money for the Simon Keith Fund to help my parents with the cost of taking care of me, such as traveling all over the country.

The downside was that the media was all over me. They had a lot of questions and wanted clear easy answers to a very complicated matter. So I looked at it as good news and bad news. Good news that I didn't need a heart right then. Bad news that I needed a heart at some point in the future. I was in limbo, wondering about when and where I'd go to get one.

One reporter asked me if I was going to ever play soccer again, and all I could say was I have to stop playing for the time being. As I answered, I looked away. I didn't want anyone to see my frustration boil over.

Over the following weeks, my parents discussed different ideas. There were hospitals at Stanford University, in Boston and at the United States National Institute for Health in Washington, D.C. All of them had great programs, but they all came with big price tags. Because the Canadian health system wouldn't cover an operation in the United States, the surgery was going to cost my family about $150,000. For a time, my parents considered selling their house.

Then came a brilliant idea from Dr. Noel Chant, my cardiologist in Victoria who was consulting my parents at that point. He had recently read an article about Dr. John Goodwin, a heart specialist in London who was considered an expert in myocarditis. Goodwin had written books on the subject and was a highly respected surgeon, and fortunately I was still an English citizen with access to British healthcare benefits. I was born there and had moved to Canada as a baby. I had also gone back just after graduating from high school to play professional and semi-professional soccer before.

Chant set up the appointment with Goodwin for May. The goal in seeing him was to get a solution. Goodwin had been doing work with a drug called interferon and Chant felt the drug might actually cure my virus so that I could avoid a transplant after all. We were ready to travel nearly 5,000 miles to get a solution and we were filled with hope and optimism. After the experience in Ontario, I was beginning to think I could avoid a transplant.

But one thing I was going to do was make sure that Goodwin saw me for the condition I was truly in. So as we prepared for the trip to England, I pulled the plug on prednisone. I wasn't going to risk suffering the same fate as what happened in Ontario, when I was hyped up on so much prednisone that I could have probably performed my own heart transplant. What I realized was prednisone was making me look too good and act too healthy. While it was helping me get through each day and live as normal a life as I could, it was masking what was really going on. If I had showed up in Ontario looking sickly and frail, maybe things would have been different.

This was my all-in play, my big gamble. To make sure Goodwin and whoever else I saw in England knew how bad I was. I weaned myself off the steroid. This was no small task. I got weak very quickly. When I took large doses of prednisone, I could generally make it through a whole day without having to take a nap. Without it, I was napping in the afternoon at first and by late morning in the days before we left for England. The drugs also helped keep me warm by making my heart feel strong enough to pump blood throughout most of my body. Without it, I was a shivering mess at the first touch of cold.

On one particularly bad day, my mom begged me to take more prednisone so that I could feel better. I refused. There was only one way to make sure the people in England knew just how bad I was and avoid an Ontario repeat. If it meant shivers, fatigue, and getting closer to death, so be it.

What I didn't realize is how big a gamble I really was taking.

We were heading off to see Goodwin for a solution, not a transplant. The prednisone had kept me as strong as possible on a day-to-day basis. But without it, I was heading towards heaven's door.

As I got to Victoria International Airport to board the flight to Gatwick International, friends and other well-wishers were there to see me off. My best friend from Sir James Douglas Elementary School, Tak Niketas, was there. I looked at him and told him I'd see him by the end of the summer. There were no tears and no fear. I was completely focused on going to England, getting fixed and coming home. I either didn't have emotions or I shut them off. Either way, they weren't present that day.

As I got on the plane, a reporter asked me if ever thought about dying. I gave one of my usual flippant answers: "Well, I won't know anything about it, will I? It's the people I leave behind that it will affect."

Truth was, I really didn't think about it. I wasn't worried about dying, I was concerned about living. I was focused on finding a solution.

So I could play the game again.

3

SOCCER PIONEERS ON THE SASKATCHEWAN TRAIL

In 1966, then-20-somethings David and Sylvia Keith were the parents of three young boys, Marc, Adam and me, who was the youngest at all of 15 months old. We were living in a new, three-bedroom house in Lewes, England. That's the idyllic part. The rest of the picture had my parents staring straight at a dead-end life.

"I was a teacher and had been for four years by then," my dad said. "The benchmark for our decision was that the man who picked up the garbage for our home was making more money than me." My dad was beginning his career as a P.E. teacher – a career he was actually encouraged to pursue by the British government. Born in 1940, he was part of what you'd call the "replacement" generation. After the loss of soldiers in World War II, there were fewer men to do certain jobs in Britain. A generation of male teachers was largely lost.

So my father was basically in the next generational group, and was given an incentive to become a teacher. He went to the University of Wales in Cardiff, now known as Cardiff University. The same Cardiff University that Robert Fields taught for much of his professional career.

By the time my father got there, the point was just to get ahead, start on a new life in a field he wanted to pursue. His passion was to become a soccer coach and a P.E. teacher.

The problem was that for all the incentives that Britain created, they missed one of the simplest points … you have to pay people a wage they can live with. That wasn't the only economic irony. As my parents considered their options, it became increasingly obvious that the best thing they could do is move to another country that was recruiting teachers.

At the time, England was led by Prime Minister Harold Wilson, a member of the Labor Party. In an effort to curb people from leaving the country, the Wilson-led government adopted a law that anyone leaving the country to live elsewhere couldn't take more than 50 pounds with them.

But my dad didn't have to worry about that.

"I didn't have 50 pounds to take with me," he said, with his typical dry British sense of humor.

"The only thing we were thinking at the time was how do we make a better life for our children?"

The answer was a drastic step. My family decided it was time to leave our homeland for a better opportunity in another country. The decision came down to Australia to the east or Canada to the west. The deciding factor was a coin flip.

The rest was not so simple.

My dad was one of four boys who grew up in a no-frills home. His father died when he was two, and his mother died when he was 13.

His stepfather was a lazy, abusive man who garnered little respect if any at all. My dad had it way tougher than me and my brothers.

He created a better life for us because he learned the value of hard work, did it himself and learned that complaining about hardship was useless. That simple, straightforward approach rubbed off on me and my brothers.

Born in Bristol, just across the Bristol Channel from Wales in the southwestern part of England, he is the third of three boys born to Henry and Phyllis Keith, both originally from Wales. Henry, an aircraft engineer, died in 1942 and my grandmother later remarried and had another son by her second marriage. When Henry Keith died, my grandmother immediately moved to Eastbourne, which is roughly three hours from Bristol on the southeastern tip of England. It's a pretty seaside resort town and she ran a hotel. That's where my father eventually met my mother, who was born and raised in Eastbourne.

As a youngster, my father grew to appreciate hard work, by watching his mother, grandfather and, in an inverted way, his stepfather. His mother worked constantly and his grandfather, who was a great man and a former miner, was an exemplary man when it came to hard work. He knew how to fix everything, and he was constantly doing whatever needed to be done.

"We had a boiler that needed coal shoveled into it constantly, and he was the one doing it. He didn't have to be asked, he understood that it needed to be done. I came to appreciate him and looked up to him."

From the sounds of it, my dad's stepfather may have been the laziest son of a gun in the world. "He never got up to do anything," my dad said. "He was always laying about, and I think subconsciously I recognized right away he was someone I didn't want to be around. So I gravitated to my grandfather, who worked hard, and away from my stepfather, the lazy one."

"To be quite frank, my stepfather was just a bully. One time, when I was about nine, he was demonstrating a wrestling move on me, and he started choking me. He didn't stop until one of my brothers came up and whacked him. He never bothered me again. I think he was afraid, really just a coward. I don't know why my mother fancied him, but after she died, he left, and I never saw him again. I don't think he even came back to see his own son. That left an impression on me: here was someone I couldn't change. I knew I couldn't change him, and I couldn't change the circumstances, so I just moved on. There wasn't any more time to waste thinking about him."

Things happened in my dad's life that patterned him. Whether it was his mom and dad dying, emulating the good example of his grandfather, or rejecting the poor example of his stepfather, it shaped his character. If you can't change something, move on.

This is what I love about my father most and what I picked up from him early in my life. The way you live your life is simple. It's like how one plus one equals two. If you know you have to do certain things to survive, you do them. You don't whine, you don't complain. You don't hesitate; you just do whatever you need to do.

Growing up, my brothers and I had dad as our coach and teacher. He didn't say much and we never felt like we could talk to him. But we didn't need to.

I spent the first 15 years of my life trying to get his respect, not knowing I had it all along. Trying to get his respect made me work harder. Just as he watched silently and learned from his grandfather as he shoveled coal into a furnace, I watched silently as my dad raised his family. I learned the value of quietly working hard. He's my mentor because he has principles, and he's got everything I stand for.

By the time my dad was 26, and facing the reality of not making enough money to raise his growing family, it was time to pick another country. This might seem drastic to some. But to my mom and dad, it was just a solution.

He went to recruiting interviews at both the Australian and Canadian offices in London, across from Trafalgar Square. The offer from Canada, which was pretty similar to what he could have gotten in Australia, was to become a teacher, in the "city" called Lestock, for a minimum of two years. The Canadian government, which was desperately in need of teachers, agreed to pay all the moving expenses, a healthy salary and other benefits in exchange for a two-year commitment from anyone who went there.

My father and mother (she went along fully, even though she had to move away from her family in Eastbourne) realize now that they didn't pick up on a few vital clues at the interview. When they asked the recruiter about Lestock, and if it was a city, the man said "sure." However, when he tried to locate it on a map, he couldn't find it. To this day, you have a hard time finding it without a lot of clues. As of the 2006 census, Lestock had a population of 138 people.

Lestock is in the Canadian Province of Saskatchewan, nestled approximately 400 miles north of the border with the United States. It's almost directly north of where Montana and North Dakota meet. Along those lines, that area of Canada is an extension of the great prairie that runs through North America from just above the Gulf of Mexico in Texas all the way to Edmonton at the north end of Canada. It is bordered by the Rocky Mountains to the west and by forests and lakes of Manitoba to the east.

It is the heartland of the continent, a robust land of farm after farm after farm. It would be an understatement to say it was desolate.

One day, in the middle of winter, my mother sent my father to the post office to check on the mail. After trudging over a couple of snow drifts, my father got there, expecting a delivery.

"The mail always arrives, right?" my father asked.

"Not in this part of the world," the postman replied.

Just getting to Lestock was the journey of a lifetime. In August, 1967 – four months before Christian Barnard performed the first heart transplant – our family packed everything it had and boarded an ocean liner bound for Montreal, Canada. From there, they would travel by train to Regina and then be driven the final two hours to lovely Lestock. Unbeknownst to my parents, my older brothers caught chicken pox just before the family got on the ship. They broke out in rashes while we were traveling, but the ship doctor refused to come see them. With each day, my parents grew increasingly edgy about not seeing the doctor -- until finally my dad hauled my brother Marc to the doc.

By this time, we were on the St. Lawrence River just outside of Quebec and just about 150 miles from Montreal, our final destination on the boat ride. My mom was going to get a first look at her new country.

Instead, this ended up being the first stop and a much longer stop than expected.

Within minutes of my mom leaving the room, the doctor and the ship security came to our room and ordered my father to pack up everything. We were going to be taken to a detention center in Quebec City. Worse, my two older brothers, aged two and four, were taken from my parents by ambulance and put in quarantine. (Later, it was explained to my father that the doctor intentionally hadn't come to our quarters because he knew he would have to put my brothers in quarantine and perhaps even send us back to England.)

Still, our problems worsened. The officials in Quebec City wouldn't listen as my parents tried to explain that it was only chicken pox.

For 10 days my brothers were detained in a hospital, as the medical experts in Quebec tried to decipher whether they had chicken pox or the much deadlier small pox.

My parents and I were held in limbo, otherwise known as a deportation center.

Technically, we weren't yet in Canada. We were still in England, of sorts. There was no communication allowed between my parents and my brothers, and no communication allowed between my parents, and the officials they were supposed to meet in Montreal and then Regina.

"Can you imagine having your children taken from you, and having no power to see them, especially when they're sick?" Still, my mom and dad were able to keep it together.

The officials had some ridiculous ideas about what would be best for my brothers. Instead of allowing my parents to check on them, they thought the strain of seeing "someone familiar" would hurt my brothers. Seriously. There were some women from the International Order of the Daughters of the Empire (IODE) who helped out. These were women from Britain, or of British descent, who lived in Quebec and normally served as a greeting committee for incoming residents. In this case, they were doing something more along the lines of a mission of mercy -- keep my parents from losing their wits.

As the days slipped by, Sept. 2, the day my father was scheduled to report for training and orientation for his new teaching job was approaching ever near. Canada was also in the middle of a train strike, which was going to impact our 1,700 mile trek from Montreal to Regina. Finally, on Sept. 1, my brothers were released. The government officials in Quebec told my parents they could go where they pleased.

"How are we supposed to do that?" my dad asked, fully aware of the train strike. When he didn't get much of an answer, he stood there ranting until finally the government officials put us on a flight at 10 p.m. to Montreal. Then, at 6 a.m. the next day, the day my father was to report for training, we boarded a flight for Regina.

Then a two-hour car ride to Lestock.

As my mother recalls, "It was over 100 degrees Fahrenheit, and the entire way to Lestock was a loose gravel road. We couldn't open the windows for all the dust."

When we finally arrived, we were all dropped off at a tiny hotel.

It wasn't as much as a hotel as a bar with rooms upstairs. Our room consisted of not much more than a shabby bed and a light hanging from the ceiling. There were no locks on the doors. The bar didn't serve food, so mom talked the woman who ran the place, Mrs. Yavinovski, into getting some milk for me.

The first night, my mom and dad awoke to the sound of a bar fight outside as one man kicked another down the stairs, screaming curse words at him. My mom remembers shaking, and even my dad had to wonder what he'd gotten us into.

From there, he started his new job in a strange place and it ended up being a completely new life.

The people of Lestock and its surrounding area were primarily of Eastern European descent, a generation or two removed in most cases. Like the Indians who were native to that area, these people were people from tough stock, having grown up in the cold climes of Europe. They had come to Canada with the promise of pretty much as much land as they could handle. As my father likes to say, some of the farms in Saskatchewan are "the size of Rhode Island." Huge tracts of flat farming land, farther than your eyes could see. The population was, at best, sparse.

This was not a city. It was barely a village. To the people of Lestock, we were more of a curiosity to them than anything.

"We were a novelty," my mom says. "We'd be talking to each other and the people would stare at us and just listen as if we were singing. They just loved to listen to our voices because they had never heard the sound of an English accent.

"After we got settled, we met some truly amazing people in Lestock. It was a true community in the sense that people helped and pitched in with everything. There aren't a lot of conveniences there, so you need each other so much. They were truly lovely to us, a very friendly group of people. It was incredible in a lot of ways because you got to know everyone.

"When we first got there, they would bring us things like a fresh-baked peach pie. Or bags and bags of corn. The thing is that I had never cooked corn before that. I had no idea what I was doing. That was the first time I ever had cabbage rolls and I learned to cook it while we were living there.

They made do with what they had and they did an incredible job of making do with it."

My mom also made the best of some very different circumstances after leaving her family in England.

Unlike my dad, my mom had an extensive family in Eastbourne. She was born Sylvia Simmons just before the start of World War II, which by today's standards would be like being born in Baghdad during the Iraq War. Eastbourne sits near the southeast tip of England, directly on the English Channel and facing France. It's roughly 70 miles south of London and, at the time, right in the middle of the flight path that German bombers used to fly on the way to London. By the end of the war, the city had been savaged by air raids and was considered the most damaged area in the southeast region of the country. Houses all over the city, including hundreds of these beautiful Victorian homes, were decimated by the war. In addition, troops were constantly stationed there for fear of invasion. Today Eastbourne is a rebuilt, charming coastal resort town.

"I remember we had an air-raid shelter in the middle of the dining room that we had to get in from time to time," my mom said. "We had soldiers staying in the house quite often."

My mom was one of five children of Henry and Ada Simmons, and, by her own account, was the "goodie two-shoes" of her family. She was a Brownie, sang in the girls' choir and attended the Anglican Church regularly.

"When (my brothers and sisters) were up to something, I was the one who stayed around the house. I was quite my father's pet. We were very close," she said.

As children, she and her siblings played relatively simple games around the house, using whatever they had for games. It could be paper cutouts for animals to pretend they had a farm, but my mother's family found a way to get along when they were young.

My mother was involved in sports, playing things like netball (an early version of basketball that was invented in England in the last 19th century). She and her friends and family would play on the chalk hills of South Downs, a beautiful and uninhabited stretch of hills that lie just to the east of

Eastbourne. That area is so pretty that England recently turned it into a national park. My mother and her friends would collect tadpoles for hours.

Inspired by her parents, the whole family would sing around the house or while romping through the Downs.

She lived in Eastbourne until she met and married my father, who by that time had moved to that part of England with his family. As my parents built a family together, they started dealing with the increasingly difficult economy in England. That's when they went to get the job offer from Canada.

" When David got the offer to teach in Saskatchewan, we went home and told my parents," she said. "My father said, 'Seeing is believing.' It was as if he had said he didn't think we could do it, which made me even more determined to do it. Coming to Canada was an incredible struggle. We thought we'd come to Canada for two years and the go back. It was hard. I was 25 and we left all our friends behind."

"The fortunate part was that we had three boys to raise, and we were so busy I didn't really notice how much I missed England until they had grown.."

Our first house was in keeping with the make-do theme.

The government purchased a condemned home in Regina and literally moved it by truck all the way to Lestock. Once they got it there, they basically plopped it down and put some wood floors right on top of the ground. There was no insulation of any kind, so you can imagine how cold it got as the earth started to freeze in the winter. The good thing is that at least we had plumbing. Many houses still got by with only an outhouse.

The rooms in the house were tiny, maybe 6-by-10 feet, so this was a long way from what my parents had given up in Lewes. That said, my father's pay raise was significant, particularly when you factored in the low expenses. My dad's first weekly salary was $411 and, and he says to this day, "I felt like I'd found the end of the rainbow." Compared to what my family was facing to make it in England, this was a huge step toward self-sufficiency.

"We went to the credit union to get a line (of credit) so we could buy furniture for the house," my mother remembered. "They gave us a $1,000 without so much as a question. I suppose they did know where to find us, but there wasn't much question. They trusted us immediately and that was refreshing, to have people who wanted to help. We took the money right away and went next door to the furniture store to get everything we needed."

Still, it was unbearably cold.

"The snow started at the end of October and didn't stop until April or May," my father said. At the time he arrived, the school was building a gymnasium. Teaching classes wasn't easy and had to be done primarily outside in the stifling cold. This is a place where children go to school with parkas, leggings and boots as standard issue and wear heavy, warm gear almost the entire day just to be somewhat comfortable.

Now think about being a P.E. teacher in that environment, trying to teach kids how to run and workout. Not exactly a conducive situation.

"It was all I could do to get them to take their parkas off," my father said. To do that, he had to set an example for them. That has always been my father's way and probably one of the reasons I take after him so much. He was a doer, not an observer.

"I never asked anyone to do something I wasn't willing to do and I never called anyone a failure," he said. It was that way during his entire run of more than 40 years as a teacher.

With that motto in mind, my dad became the "Crazy Englishman of Lestock." He started small. During classes, as the temperature progressively dipped into the 30s and then the 20s, my father would conduct class in a t-shirt, gym shorts and "runners," or what we now call sneakers. And remember, sneakers back in the 1960s weren't the sophisticated shoes of today. We're talking about the bare-bones, Chuck Taylor-autographed versions that kids wear now as a sign of retro-fashion.

"I had to set the example of how we were going to do this. It was just about freezing, and I told them they had to get out there. When I told them the only way to get a passing grade was to go outside, they finally seemed to really understand. They still looked at me a bit like I was crazy, but that was fine. They got outside and started to really breathe deep and break a little sweat, even in the cold. This was extremely elementary fitness teaching, but that's what they needed to get," he said.

As for the "crazy" part, my dad took it one step further to make his point to the whole community. We lived about a block and a half from school, down the street of a row of houses of Eastern European ex-patriots who didn't quite know what to make of this British family and its patriarch. My dad confused them further by sprinting to work each day – each and every day - regardless of the weather.

There were times when Lestock would drop to 10 or even 20 degrees below zero. If there was a good breeze that day, the wind chill would sink to negative-30 or even negative-40. Still, there was my dad, running to school.

In a t-shirt, shorts and gym shoes.

"I would have won the Olympic gold medal in the sprints back then," he said. As he ran, the women in the houses would look at him, perhaps wondering if he was mentally fit enough to be teaching their children. If nothing else, he made his point and the students followed along.

Things did improve during the two years. My parents started renting a nice home from the local representative to the regional government. Even though it was a duplex, it was a far better home with a better rental price. At one point, my father even put money down to buy a home in Lestock, but then got a job offer to go to Victoria, British Columbia. The trek across Canada – and really across the world – was going to take us another 1,200 miles west.

"We kept saying, 'It's just for two years.' We kept saying that with the intention we would go back to England," said my mom, who missed her family terribly. "But you get busy with your life and raising your children and then you set down roots and the next thing you know, you've been somewhere for 20 years."

As my dad explained: "We knew we couldn't stay in Lestock, even though the people were wonderful. There wasn't enough opportunity and you knew that the school would be limited to what it could offer. You have to understand, even with the Indian children who were bused to the school every day, the graduating class from the school my first year was eight students. By the next year, we had a huge jump to 12. There wasn't going to be the opportunity for the kind of education we wanted for our children."

In the years to come, David became a widely respected coach and teacher in Victoria, a community that would come to love and appreciate his sick son.

But in those early years in Lestock, really what they had set in motion was the willingness and courage to do whatever it took to succeed.

It's a trait that became crucial to my core beliefs.

4

GROWING UP A KEITH

I spent my childhood looking up, literally and figuratively. I was about 4-foot-nothing for most of my life, not growing much until I was in high school. All the while, I was trying to compete with two brothers who were not only bigger than me, but also, in my estimation, always better athletes. Then there was my father, this silent, powerful, driven man who doled out approval with sparing brilliance. Behind the scenes was mom, the unsung hero living a glamourless life as a wife and mother to four athletes.

As an adult, I pride myself on having what I call a "laser focus" on my goals. Once I establish what I want to do, I don't let go of that focus for a moment. Whether it has been to play soccer again after my heart transplant, or to make money, or be a good husband and father, I am able to accomplish my goals because I don't let other factors get in my way. I don't get distracted, or head off on some other path.

Some people say you have to be born with this skill. In my opinion, it's developed. At least it was for me. It was developed by constantly trying to compete with my brothers and in search of praise from my father.

Coaches often tell you that the youngest child in a family has a tendency to become the best athlete of the bunch. New England quarterback Tom Brady is the youngest of four kids. His three siblings were all girls, but they were all great athletes. His sisters played softball and he grew up playing catch with his dad.

In the great Manning family, it may turn out that Eli – the youngest -- may actually be the best of three brothers, which is an amazing thing considering how good his brother Peyton has been.

When you're the youngest, it's the natural battle to keep up, whether it's with your brothers or with all their buddies they're playing with. With me, I wasn't just trying to keep up with my brothers, I was trying to knock them off the pedestal I put them on. We fought a few times, although somewhat comically. Compared to my brothers (middle brother Adam was 5-foot-8 by the time he was 13 or 14) I was a runt, constantly trying to fight them.

"Simon was 5-2 in 11th grade and I was 5-7 in 7th grade, if that puts it in perspective for you," Adam said. "We'd fight all around the house, literally, we'd wrestle or punch each other. But mostly it was Simon trying to hit one of us. I would just giggle at him, and that made him madder because it was like I was mocking him. The more I giggled, the madder he would get."

"Tenacious? He's the definition of tenacity. I can't say that made him survive his situation, but it didn't hurt him. Really, what it made him most was competitive, extremely competitive. He wouldn't back down from anything. Here's this little guy pushing himself as hard as he could all the time to keep up with us. He says we were better athletes. Maybe when we were young. But he had this incredible drive."

All the way to the breakfast table. The Keith boys would compete over everything, right down to who had more cereal left in their bowl in the morning.

"We'd look at each other and say, 'How much have you got left?' One of us would say, 'I have more than you.' Even though the cereal was covered by milk, now it was a competition to see who had more cereal. We'd just sit there staring at each other trying to prove who had more. You look back at it and it doesn't make any sense. You're supposed to eat the cereal and just move on for the rest of the day, you know? Not us. Everything was a competition. ," Adam said. "It would drive our mother a little crazy at times, but our dad understood."

I don't remember the fights being so constant, but I do know Adam made me madder than hell when he was laughing at me while I tried to punch him. "Just because you're the biggest and the loudest doesn't make you right," I would yell at the top of my voice.

Being in this situation set in motion that focus I have today. There's nothing I wanted more than to be better than Adam and Marc, with the possible exception of the need for the praise of my father.

Adam was a great soccer player. From the time he was four or five, he was just a beast. He was the kid that took every throw-in, every goal kick, every free kick, every penalty kick. When he became a teenager, he was a monster. He was all-everything. At 15, he was playing on men's teams in one of the best amateur leagues in North American at the time and he didn't just hold his own, he dominated. I can't begin to explain how high the bar was set by Adam. Marc was a very, very good player but because he was four years older me it felt like a different deal. I played on *Adam's team*. It wasn't that we played on the same team, it was *his* team, so I saw how good he was every day. It wouldn't be exaggerating to say Adam was one of the best players in Canada from age 14 to 18. He was better than most men.

It was Adam, in fact, who got me the chance to play at the University of Nevada-Las Vegas (UNLV). In many ways I followed in Adam's footsteps in most of my athletic career. This started early and continued throughout my life.

With Marc, he was a really good player too, but he was also the smartest of us all. He got straight A's all the time. I always remember thinking that I had to do everything possible to keep up with both of them. It was not an occasional thought. It was imprinted on the front of my brain as I grew up. Not in a bad way, but I felt like I was always an afterthought. When we would go to Marc's practice. Adam and I would tag along. Sometimes Adam would practice with them, but I couldn't because I was too small. When we went to "our" team practice, it was really all about Adam because he dominated so much. In many ways I felt invisible. I was always trying to get noticed. Always.

I had to be a great athlete and a great student and I never thought I measured up on either one. My desire to keep up and be competitive with them was important for me because it was natural. It wasn't like I was ever compared to them by my parents. It was just how I felt inside. We were all good in soccer and we played because we loved it, not because we were forced to do it. Later on, even after Marc had left for college, I remember being reminded of the importance of school. By then I had started to dream that maybe, just maybe, I might be able to get drafted into the pro leagues. It was a long shot, but kids can dream.

The important thing for me was that I had this really strong connection to my brothers. I wanted to be like them so badly that it drove me and drove me. That's not the same anymore because we all do different things as adults. But I firmly believe that my ability to succeed is based on how much I pushed myself to keep up with my brothers. They were the measuring stick to me when I was little. I looked up to them in every way. Anything they did, I wanted to try. When I was 11 or 12, I would come home everyday after school and practice and practice and practice.

Growing up, there was this thing call the Adidas Competition. It was a series of six tests on soccer skills, much like the Presidential Physical Fitness tests. There was a shuttle run you did with the ball, a shooting test, a heading test, the whole gamut. The idea was to keep kids practicing using measurable goals and have club, then city, then province and then, finally, the national competitions. My favorite test was the juggling test. Keep the ball off the ground using only your feet or thighs for as many as you can up to 300 all while staying inside the center circle of a soccer field.

Adam was a natural, no surprise. He would literally never practice once, pick up the ball at 12 years old and knock out 150 juggles. I would – usually in silence – vow to beat him even while being stuck at some ridiculous number like 13. I would practice every day for hours on end – while Adam was messing around with friends, watching TV or whatever. Finally after weeks of practice I would rush into the house and declare, "I have broken the record, I got 176!!!" I was jacked up. I thought I was the best in the house.

Adam would walk outside and, after not practicing one, single, stinking time since the last time he did it, pick the ball up and promptly do 223.

Annoying? Yes. Motivating? Yes. Building an internal drive for me? Definitely.

When we went to the competition, I survived the club level to earn the right to compete for the city title. Adam was the other representative from our club. In the city finals I came in maybe 12th. Adam won. Off to the provincial level. Adam won. Off to the national competition. He messed up and came second. Yep, no biggie, just another day for me living in a huge shadow. Adam and I always talk about this event today. I really truly consider it an advantage having grown up in his shadow. Who knew it would be to my advantage to be the FOURTH best player in my house?

I always thought Adam was going to be the professional soccer player, not me. I just followed him around, hoping to pick up something, learn whatever I could. I dreamed of playing pro soccer, but it was just a dream. In reality, I thought I was going to be a P.E. teacher just like my dad.

As we got older, our styles changed a little bit. Adam stayed very consistent. He was always a very central player who had great vision, great ability to distribute the ball and toughness in a tackle. As he got older, he tended to play a little deeper in midfield. As I got older, I became more focused on going forward. I was interested in taking players on and attacking the goal. In fact, many of my former coaches and teammates will attest that defending was a kind of four-letter word for me. I never had a problem taking a shot, even if I missed 50 in a row. I had the confidence that I was going to make the next one.

I wanted to go forward all the time, attack, not sit back and wait for the action to come to me. That's just how my brain works. I'm aggressive, always pushing and pushing and pushing. I think there's an important distinction there for me. My competition with my brothers was never really a competition because it was so lopsided. I was never jealous of them. I always wanted them to be great. I looked up to them and their friends. Secretly, I just wanted to be better. I wanted to be pushed by their success, not have them be mediocre.

I have a big ego, and I know it. I always wanted people to say to me, "You're a great guy, a great player, you're the best on the field." I wanted to be the best among the best players and that started at home. I wouldn't be here today if it wasn't for them pushing me.

I wouldn't be here either if it weren't for my parents. My mother always provided the support we need to succeed in academics and sports. It doesn't sound glamorous but if we needed food it was there, if we needed our gear it was there, if we need help on our schoolwork she was there. This is the role she took and she played it to perfection as we grew up.

My father was a stern teacher. He was our P.E. teacher and pretty much our coach at every level. He wasn't always literally the coach, but he always had a hand in how our teams were run and who the coach was. He made sure we were with coaches who he thought were going to teach us what we needed at that time.

It is quite a leap of faith when you know inside that you are an excellent coach, maybe the best in the area, and it is time to hand your kids over to someone else. My dad understood that at times in our development, it was better for us to be coached by others. The coaches we had met his very stringent criteria.

When we were young kids he entrusted our development with guys like Jon McGuire, Steve Forslund and then later Grant Darley and Tiberio DeFrias.

Forslund was a diminutive, yet tough, forward who played on the famed Vic West through its heyday as national champions. During exhibition matches against visiting pro teams, he would routinely best his marking defender and launch missiles across the box. McGuire, also of VicWest, was no less impressive. A former member of the Canadian youth team and a pure soccer player. These guys were amateurs, but you match them up against the pros, and you'd think they got the line-ups mixed up.

Darley was an impressive keeper who played at the highest levels, including the professional ranks, and played a big role in my personal development. DeFrias has soccer in his veins. And these guys all had one thing in common. They were tough, hard-workers who were not easily impressed. They could teach kids the game, or a key part of the game, largely by their example, with few words.

These were the coaches of my very young days. I had many, many very good and important coaches in my teen and later years. People like Mike Deturbeville, and Ian Franks, Brian Hughes, Bruce Twamley, Bruce Wilson, Barrie Clark. I could literally name 50. All were vitally important to my development…but it is the coaches that I had when I was very young, when fundamentals and work ethic were being ingrained in me that proved to be so important.

Years later, when I ended up earning spots playing on teams with these guys it always felt surreal. My Dad was always about finding coaches who taught strong fundamentals and had a firm approach. It wasn't about us playing for coaches who were going to favor us.

My dad always believed that the less he said, the better. In high school, everybody thought he was as tough as a dad as he was as a coach. He wasn't loud or obnoxious, he was just really direct. He told you what the expectation was, showed you how to do it and then let you do it. If you didn't, you got "the look." My dad didn't mess around with people, he got to the point. The other kids at school used to say, "Oh, your dad must make you do pushups and sit-ups at home all night." It wasn't that way at all. In fact, my mom was probably more demanding of us at home when it came to getting things done.

My dad is my mentor because he has the same core principles and that I stand for. He wouldn't give us a lot of empty praise. There wasn't much, "You're doing great," if you were just doing OK. There wasn't this big rah, rah thing if you were just doing the normal thing that was expected of you. Coaches like the great Bobby Robson or Sir Alex Ferguson used to ask their players rhetorical questions like, "You want praise for working hard? Isn't that what you're supposed to be doing?"

Some people take that the wrong way. They think, "Well, screw it if he's not going to say anything about how I'm doing." I was just the opposite. I was looking for some way that I could get him to give me that praise. I craved it and would do any amount of hard work to get it. I understand the idea that you're not just supposed to hold people's hands all the time and give them fake praise. At the same time, my father wasn't sitting there ripping people, either. It was never negativity, it was about creating a standard.

I never realized it at the time, but I had been watching this happen for years. As a 5 or 6 year old my Dad had a great team at the Victoria Boys Club. The basis of the great Vic West teams in the 1970's and 80's came from that Boys Club team. He instilled discipline in a group of young men that didn't know at the time they needed it.

"You knew what was expected of you and the rest of the people on the team," said Ian Bridge, a player from the Island who made it in the big leagues.

I experienced that in school when I went to Central Junior High School. But I really saw it first hand in the 10th grade. I had begun training with a men's senior amateur team in Victoria that my Dad coached. You could make a very strong argument that soccer in Victoria and Vancouver in the 70s and 80s was the best league in the country and one the top in all of North

America. We didn't realize this at the time, but it was a tremendous time to be part of the soccer culture in Victoria and all of British Columbia. The Prospect Lake Lakers were a group of mostly misfits and cast offs that my dad coached. I say this in the nicest way possible, but no one was going to mistake them for the best players available in a soccer rich environment. When I trained with them each Tuesday and Thursday night, I was my regular self. Quiet, small, and in the shadow.

But I was perceptive. Until then, I had never been around a team that worked as hard. My Dad simply ran these guys into the ground. Day after day after day. He quietly went about driving these "undesirables" into a something far greater than the sum of their parts. These were 20- to 35-year-old men with full-time jobs such as working at Pepsi or as a weddings DJ. They had wives and kids and responsibilities, and yet they pledged their allegiance to this strict disciplinarian who made them work till they had nothing left.

And they loved it!

It was one of those moments for me when I really understood what a gift my Dad was and what a gift soccer is.

Soccer, too, has a heart; and what I was seeing was the heart of the game.

My dad was, and still is, the very best soccer coach I have ever been around. He was years ahead of his time. He was an incredibly successful provincial coach and even participated at the National World Cup level with the Canadian World Cup Team. Those that played for him would run through walls for him. Those that played against him hated him. This is the gold standard of coaching.

As a Dad, sometimes the line between father and coach– only in my mind, never in his – got crossed. There was one time in 11th grade when I thought he was going to really praise me. I was in the British Columbia high school championship for Mount Douglas. We had a very good, close-knit team and I'm still friends with many of the guys from the team. I was one of only three juniors on the team and I had never really distinguished myself before, although other people were starting to quietly tell me I was starting to play well. We finished third in British Columbia, which was a disappointment because we felt we had the best team. The cool surprise for me was I made the first all-star team. I had played a great tournament and for the very first time in my life I had won an award while playing on a team with Adam. It may have been 9,000 to 1 for Adam in terms of accolades, but that was irrelevant. I was proud of what I had accomplished. I came home and thought, man, this was going to clinch it. My dad is really going to praise me.

Nothing.

He didn't say a word.

Nada, zilch.

I kind of broke down at that moment, and said: "What's the deal here? I put in all this work out there, I finally do something right, something really great, and I don't get any response. I get nothing."

He just kind of stared at me and I sort of go. at that moment. I realized that's how he was going to be because that's how he had been with Marc and Adam. He didn't just throw praise around to them and if he didn't do it for them, he wasn't going to do it for me. He had to be consistent. If he wasn't consistent, he was asking for trouble. It was another view into my dad's genius.

Having him as our P.E. teacher wasn't that big a deal because we were always the best in the class. He didn't have to tell us what to do over and over again. To be honest, it probably kept me in line more from a subconscious side than him having to say or do anything. I went to Central, which wasn't the greatest school in the world. There would be fights and stupid things going on. I stayed away from that for the most part because I knew that if I ever did the wrong thing, my dad would let me have it.

When he was still teaching and coaching, he would get this great joy from going places where people didn't really know him. He knew he could have more of an impact on the game if he coached the coaches instead of trying to coach lots of players. He spent 40 years dedicated to trying to teach others to coach.

At Central, whenever the principal would be out of school for a day or so, my father was put in charge. Or he would be called in to deal with discipline issues when the principal wasn't around. He spent 34 years as a teacher at Central and there was a depth of purpose to how he did his job.

As my dad explained it: "The staff would keep their worst discipline problems for me, because they knew they would be dealt with fairly and there would be follow-up. I would find out what was going on with the students. I had a set of principles that I followed. First of all, I was always more concerned with ethics and morals than the end results. It was about the process of how students got there. From there, it was about being consistent, setting standards and then getting students to accept there are certain things they must do and certain things they cannot do."

People recognized my father's presence from the time he got there. One of our friends from the neighborhood was Hans de Goede. He was older than all of the boys in my family. He was in eighth grade when we moved there. He was at Central Junior High and later went on to play rugby for 13 years, going from Canada to England and other parts of the world. In fact, he was the captain of Canada's team in the first rugby World Cup in 1987. He is regarded as Canada's greatest rugby player of all time and one of the finest to ever play the game in the world. At 6-foot-4 and 225 pounds as an eighth grader de Goede was an intimidating student.

"David was a specimen," de Goede said. "Although he wasn't tall, he was a very fit, physical gentleman and a superb soccer player. Most of us played youth soccer, so we all thought we were pretty good, but he would just run circles around us to make a point when he taught. He was a wizard on the pitch. He coached us and he had a presence about him, a sense of authority. We never felt intimidated by him, it wasn't that. He was just a person who you weren't going to talk back to. It was a good, healthy, respectful relationship that you look back on as you get older and admire."

With us, it was exactly like that the entire time. My dad wanted us to be prepared by the situations we had been through, good, bad or indifferent. His goal was to build people who could lead, who would be able to take control of situations. To me, that meant taking care of myself first. Being involved in sports made a lot of that easy. If you're on the field all the time and then you're taking care of school, there's not much time left for stupidity.

There's more to it than just that. These days, I talk to my son Sean all the time about surrounding himself with people who want to do things the right way. In high school, you have all sorts of temptations, whether they are alcohol, recreational drugs and now performance enhancing stuff like steroids.

You have to have a group of people around you who want to make good choices, people you can feel good about being around.

From the time I was in elementary school at Sir James Douglas, my best friend was Takie "Tak" Niketas. We stayed friends all the way through high school and have been like brothers since. When other people were doing some stupid stuff, Tak and I didn't have to do that just to fit in, to feel like we belonged.

If we went to party, I knew he would have my back if things started going south. The fact that he also happened to have a ham-and-swiss or turkey-on-rye sandwich with him at all times was a bonus. Seriously, Tak had a sandwich with him all the times. In his pocket, in his car, in his hockey bag … all the time. It was just one of those funny quirks that makes a him unique….different.

Not that we didn't get into mischief. Here is a typical "party" story for me and Tak. It was a Saturday night and we were in 10th grade. There was a beach party we knew about but we decided to go the local junior hockey game. Usually it was three of us, with Ian Klitise, another of my very closest boyhood friends with us but on this night it just me and Tak. The Victoria Cougars were a very good junior hockey team at the time and we were just beginning to see players close to our age play for them. The Cougars were part of the Junior A system in Canada. For the elite players the next stop was the NHL.

After the game, we were walking home. It was maybe 10 p.m. and we pass a semi-famous place called the Beacon Drive-In. They serve ice cream, root beer floats and all that dessert stuff. The place was closed, but we noticed that the freezer in the back was open. Low and behold there is a carton of eggs. Not a 12-pack. No, a carton of with rows of 24. There must have been six or eight rows, somewhere between 150 and 200 eggs.

So here we are with all these eggs at our disposal and we come up with the bright idea to go to the beach party. As we approach the party, it is down a cliff off of Dallas Road and maybe 50 feet below us. Bombs away! We are in hysterics as we just throw egg and after egg at the party goers below. It takes the people below a few minutes to understand what is happening and that's when we high tailed it out of there.

The next Monday at school, we could hardly contain ourselves as the story of the egging made its way around school.

This was pretty typical of how Tak and I liked to party. I didn't dislike anybody, I just didn't have time or desire to do drugs or drink or party all the time. I was indifferent to stuff like that. I would say to those people: "Go ahead, do what you want. Just don't expect me to jump on the bandwagon and say you're a great guy. Do whatever you want. Don't worry about what I may think about you. I don't worry about what other people think of me."

Tak was the same way. He never cared what other people thought about him. That's probably why we get along so well. We do what we want to do, not what other people think we should do. When we were growing up, if that meant going skating on a Friday night instead of going to the big party, that's what we would do. Before we got to be really tight around eighth grade, I used to be part of this group of jocks. There were like six or seven guys and we used to hang out and do things that I didn't like. Like you had to walk in the group of seven guys. You couldn't just hang out with one or two of the other guys, it always had to be this big production and it just felt dumb. I felt like all those guys were sheep and that's not how I viewed myself.

Tak was an unbelievably close friend for me. He was instrumental in getting me so much help from the community. My dad always told me, "If you find one really true friend in your life, you've done well." Tak is that guy. He has always been there for me and always will be. Likewise, me for him. When I got sick, he was unreal. I think he raised $7,000 by himself to help me and my family when the expenses were getting so outrageous. I have other friends who are similar from my playing days. Guys I have known for 30 or 40 years and are as close to as friends can be. But no one is really like Tak. He even spent time with me when I got sick and couldn't really do anything anymore. We'd play cards or shoot pool. Nothing physically strenuous, but he helped keep my mind off things and it beat the hell out of watching TV.

I'm not saying I was an angel. I had my share of beers at parties. But there was never anything crazy and nothing really illegal. In school, we did some mischievous stuff, but never real trouble. The point is that I was never going to take it too far. We were never going to do anything truly stupid because we knew where the line was drawn. The mother of one of my friends used to say this about me, "You have to know to leave the party before trouble starts." That was the real trick, and Tak and I had it down.

The closest I ever came to getting in trouble is when Tak and I went out to steal a bicycle one time. I'm not proud of this. It was a silly dare. It was probably when we were in eighth grade. We got the bright idea because Tak found some bolt cutters, so we thought we could find a nice bike and clip the lock. So we put on some clothes we normally didn't wear and we rode my bike down to the provincial museum where there was this nice bike. It was perfect, except that it was up against this window that was mirrored on one side. In other words, we couldn't see in, but the people on the inside could see us clear as day. So we're standing there trying to cut the lock, but it won't cut because the bolt cutters are like 15 years old and really dull. What a pair of criminal masterminds we were!

All of a sudden, from out of the museum comes this businessman with his pant leg tucked into his socks from riding his bike, a bike clip on and a briefcase in his hand. He just starts running after us. I jumped on my bike and started riding and Tak just started running with me. Then the chain on my bike fell off and I had to just grab my bike and run while this businessman chased us. I'm glad my mom never heard about that one. She really would have killed me for that. So much for our life of crime.

We did have some guys who were ready for trouble. When we were in eighth grade, we had this one little guy who was always doing something wrong. His name was Rudolpho. I have no idea where he is today. We're playing basketball one day and he comes driving up in a car. We're maybe 14 years old and here comes this little guy driving. He put boxes on the accelerator and the brake just so he could push the pedals with his feet. You could barely see his head over the steering wheel. He drives up and says, "Hey guys, let's go." He had stolen the car and wanted to go for a ride. We were like, "Dude, take it back where you found it." That was nothing but trouble.

Rudolpho also was the guy who hooked all the poor kids up with great shoes, the Nike Air high tops or whatever they were. They were the leather basketball shoes that went for probably $110 a pair. Again, we're in maybe ninth grade and he would go down to Hudson's Bay Company store and steal a pair of shoes every day and then sell them to the guys on the basketball team for $20 each. Our entire team at Central had the best basketball shoes.

To me, I got more out of testing the limits of my body and playing sports. When we had fitness tests in school, I loved it. Back in sixth and seventh grade, I had this friend Dave Backhouse. We used to get to school at 6 in the morning and see how far we could run. We would try to run 10 miles sometimes before school starts. It was crazy stuff. When you're a kid, you don't understand that's not the right thing to do before you start school.

At Central I spent two years playing soccer virtually every day after school and on the weekends with Ian Klitsie. Ian was a year older than me and we too got into some trouble but nothing crazy. We were more interested in kicking a ball around than going to the party…although it would not be accurate to say we didn't go to parties. We just knew that we wanted to play first, and everything else fell a distant second.

That all relates to the lessons my dad instilled in us and the goals I had were reinforced by having two great older brothers I could look up to and emulate. Not just emulate, but want to be better than, in a healthy, competitive way.

The final ingredient to this mix was soccer. I always knew I was an OK player, although small for my age. But I loved the game. When I was in third grade, I was already playing on the seventh grade team. My teacher, Mrs. Steel, wouldn't let me go until I showed her my homework. As a third grader, homework was something I couldn't understand. One day, I was in a hurry to get to my game, and she asked for my homework. "I've got to go to the game," I shouted and threw my book at her. I wasn't trying to hurt her, but it was like, "Here you go, here's my work." I think my parents had to come to school to deal with that one. Mrs. Steel didn't like that very much.

But I didn't think I had what it took to be special. At least not until I made that first all-star team in the British Columbia Championships. After that, I got a phone call to come out for the National Youth Team. The Canadian National Youth Team was calling me! I could hardly believe it. Little did I know that the situation was tailor-made for me. I was one of the youngest guys on the team, playing against some guys who were a year or two older than me. It was fantastic competition for me because it reinforced so much of what I had already dealt with growing up with my brothers. Only this time I had grown a bit and I was finally prepared to come out of the shadows.

5

THE BEAUTIFUL GAME

Some people might look at my story and wonder: Why was it so important for you to play soccer? I had made it to the top once, only to have everything I had worked for ripped out from under me. After I had a heart transplant, why do it again? Most people would probably have called it a day after that.

But soccer is my passion, and it has been from the time I was little boy.

There's a line from a Pearl Jam song that goes, "All that's sacred comes from youth."

Soccer is sacred to me. As a boy and as a young man, it was my faith and my church. It was a vehicle to teach me lessons, and to put me on a path to the life I have now.

In other words, I owe the game a lot more than it owes me.

Soccer has been ever present in my life from the time I was three or four years old and playing alongside Adam at the Victoria Boys Club. From there, I moved up through the youth soccer system. I was a city all-star, a provincial representative, a top amateur involved with the Canadian national program, a college player in two countries and finally a professional in England, Canada and the United States.

For me, the game is like a treadmill that speeds up every so often. You either speed up with it or you fall off. The trick in developing as a player is to embrace this increased pace. You have to remain humble as the speed changes while at the same time keeping your confidence high that you will be able to keep up.

But it was about more than simply playing. It was about dreams and aspirations. Soccer wasn't just something I played as a little kid. It was something I dreamed about *doing* for my life. When you get a hint of how great that dream can be, you want to chase it as far as you can. That moment for me was when I was 11 years old and still impressionable. For the first time in my life, I went to a North American Soccer League game and I got a chance to see my heroes up close and personally.

The NASL started in 1968. The league raced out of the gate with more than 15 teams, then stumbled and almost folded many times until 1975, when it got back up to its original number of 15. I was 10 in 1975 when I really started to notice the league. Maybe it was because the Vancouver Whitecaps entered the league in 1974 and I now had a home team to cheer for. More likely, it was because in 1975 Pele arrived in New York. The game was now "big time" to those of us who loved soccer. There were sellout crowds in New York and the game was shown on network TV.

Closer to home, my boyhood idol, Ian Bridge, was playing a couple of hundred miles away for the Seattle Sounders. As an impressionable little boy, the NASL gave me and so many other kids a stage on which we all hoped to perform on one day.

Watching the Cosmos on TV was cool, but the lasting imprint was when I went to see them for the first time in-person. I got a chance to watch the Cosmos play my Vancouver Whitecaps at old Empire Stadium in Vancouver. The place was demolished back in 1993, but it held just over 32,000 people in its heyday and it was my field of dreams.

The Cosmos had Pele still and other stars like Franz Beckenbauer and Georgio Chinaglia. The Whitecaps had now familiar players such as Bobby Lenarduzzi and Carl Valentine. In later years, the talented Peter Beardsley played for Vancouver. He was one of my all-time favorites and later went on to represent England in the World Cup in Mexico in 1986.

On top of just being there, I was on a city all-star team that was selected to play an exhibition match during halftime. This was epic stuff for a little kid. We made the ferry ride to the promised land of Empire Stadium. One of the ironies of the day is that Jeff Mallett was a teammate of mine on that all-star team. Mallet was a great player and one of Canada's top youth prospects. Years later, Mallet and NBA superstar Steve Nash went on to buy the Whitecaps.

When our all-star team finally got to step on the field, it was amazing. I played right wing in those days, setting up way outside because I was one of the smaller kids on the team and playing with guys who were older. The coaches didn't want me to get overwhelmed by the bigger guys. But as I stood on the right sideline, the crowning of the field (that's done to make sure the field drains properly when it rains) was so steep that I couldn't see what was happening on the other side. I had no idea where the ball was. On top of that, the "turf" was rock hard. All the field seemed to be was a layer of green pool felt laid on top of cement. You didn't want to slide or fall on that stuff. It seemed so bizarre to me.

But it was thrilling. The stadium was filled to capacity and even though half the crowd had probably filed out to the concessions or the bathrooms for halftime, it felt like all 32,000 of them were staring at us. That was electric stuff.

After our exhibition, we stood as the Whitecaps and the Cosmos came back out for the second half. It was the first time I had seen a professional soccer player in the flesh. They were like rock stars. Flowing hair, huge legs, and they all looked tough and mean. I couldn't imagine ever being that big or that cool. I could imagine my brother Adam making it that far. He was a rock star with the flowing-hair persona. It totally made sense that he would one day become a pro. For me, I couldn't see anyone who looked like me. There was no real runt on the field.

In the second half, we sat in the crowd as the fans on one side of the stadium kept yelling "WHITE!" at the top of their lungs and the other side would yell "CAPS!" This seemed to go on for the entire second as I screamed "CAPS!" the entire time. The whole place was totally into it.

After the game, we were able to go back on the field and wait for the players to come out of the locker room. We got autographs from our new idols. They signed soccer balls, pennants, jackets … anything and everything. My first professional autograph came from … Pele.

Awesome.

As I travelled back to Victoria I was on cloud nine. I was a fan. I was in complete and total awe, never imaging that I could one day be like one of those guys. No way, not a chance. Adam? Yes. Me? Never.

Prior to the NASL, the game was basically left to immigrants. Around Canada or the United States, wherever you had pockets of people from some place in Europe or some other place where soccer was big, you would have teams pop up. These were amateur teams and the names usually reflected the heritage of the players. You'd have the Greek-Americans team or Team Italia in cities across the country. That kept the game as a niche sport for the first half of the 20th century.

During the 1950s and 1960s, there were some hotbeds for the game. St. Louis, Toronto, San Francisco, Philadelphia and different towns all over New Jersey had more and more serious players and they developed company teams that eventually would play for what they called "national" championships. It wasn't much different than how teams were formed back in England or in the early days of leagues like the NFL (the Green Bay Packers were a company team when they got started).

The reality is there really wasn't a "national" level of organization. The tournaments were regionalized. The players were passionate, dedicated and set the stage for the NASL, which set the stage for guys like me to love the sport and take it even further. The NASL was the Golden Age of the game to guys in my age group.

The sad part is that getting people into soccer enough to sustain the game in the late 70's and early 80's was too hard. I vividly remember the fall of the NASL. In 1982, I was playing for the British Columbia provincial 18-and-under team and we were set up for a match that day against our 17-and-under team. It was just a practice match, but my coach told me before the game that a scout from the Fort Lauderdale Strikers was going to be there that day to watch me. Me? "Yeah, YOU," he said. I was making steady progress in my game to that point, but this day ended up being one where I took a stride instead of a step.

The younger team bolted to a 2-0 lead by halftime and we were playing poorly. Losing to the young team just wasn't cutting it. I had been playing in the center of mid-field and doing just OK. At halftime – and for the very first time in my life – I asked the coach if I could play up front. Up to then, I liked to play just behind a big man (or a couple of bigger guys) and pick up loose balls and attack the defense with pace. I had never had the courage to ask a coach to play me in a position other than what he thought was best. But for some reason, I just felt strongly that day.

From that day on, I never really played any other position. I had an absolutely dominant second half. I scored three goals, we came back and won, 4-3, and everything I did was right. At the end of the game, the coach sat the team down and he actually told the other players on my team to thank me for saving their asses against the younger team. I felt, for the first time in my life, that I was the best player on a field filled with elite players. It was a very strange feeling. I had never been in the top three players *in my* house, so now my confidence was soaring.

I couldn't wait to talk to the scout. I knew had a real chance to make an impression. I asked the coach where the scout was and he unsympathetically told me that he had left at halftime. This wasn't just bad luck for me; it was an indicator of things to come. The league continued on. And it continued to come closer to me than ever before. A friend of mine from high school, Brian Mousely, got drafted by the Portland Timbers when I was in 11th grade. Brian -- or Moser as he was affectionately called by many -- had an amazing work ethic and love for the game. He came from a hard-working family and from a very early age had developed a professional outlook towards the game.

NASL rules at the time were that most teams fielded only three North American-born players. The rest of the slots went to highly-paid internationals who came to America to ply their trade. So it was out of thousands and thousands of young players that Moser had made it into the big leagues.

There were rumors that teams were looking at me too. I actually talked to a New York Cosmos scout. They said they were interested. The same team that I had watched seven years earlier at my first professional game wanted me? *The* New York Cosmos. I couldn't believe it.

Then, suddenly, it was all gone. The NASL folded, just like that. Our dreams popped like a bubble.

We kept on playing though, because we had a heart for the game. Brian eventually earned a spot on a professional team in Calgary, and was the heart of the team until that league folded as well.

There were, and still are, many theories as to why the NASL collapsed. I didn't care then and I am not sure I care now. All I know is that I was devastated. The league that was so tantalizing close, was gone. But I had the sense enough to know there was life beyond soccer. I wasn't so wrapped up in the dream that I didn't understand reality. Still, this stung. It was a gigantic tease.

The fall of the NASL started what is commonly known as the "Dark Decade" of soccer in North America. For players in my generation, we had to scrap and fight to find high-level soccer.

The MISL allowed me the chance to play pro soccer in the United States and chase my dream a little further. The MISL was not what so many of us grew up watching with the NASL. It was an indoor game played at amazing pace, a non-stop sprint that required an incredible amount of fitness. And the fans loved it. Many of the world's best from the NASL made the transition to the indoor league. It truly was an amazing experience, and I was well-suited for the game.

The United States had some other "professional" leagues at the time and the Canadian Soccer League was around. I had my couple of seasons in the CSL, but it was really a disjointed mess. The careers of players who were in their prime during this decade suffered. Some of us went to England and that was a great adventure for me when I was just out of high school. The Canadian National Program started off great for me, too. Still, it was never about being in one place and in one league long enough to really develop. It was hopscotching from one place to the next and that can wear you out mentally, if not physically. Throw in my heart transplant and I was a recipe for burnout by the early 1990s. I don't blame anybody or anything, it was just my reality.

Underneath all of that, however, I still have a passion for the game. It was still what created so many wonderful, passionate moments in my life. The friendships I have from playing are forever. The funny stories, the glorious moments, even the frustration and heartache (no pun intended); it was all there for me to take in and help make me the person I am today.

Fortunately, Federation Internationale de Football Association (FIFA), decided that the 1994 World Cup would be hosted by the United States.

FIFA did that on one condition: That a domestic league had to be put in place.

The 1994 World Cup was magical. It was a chance to see real soccer in our own country. Tickets seemed plentiful at first, but then a real scramble ensued. It was going to be difficult to see any games except meaningless ones in the early rounds. Of course, I wanted to go to the final. I called everyone I knew. I called in every favor. I figured that I would be able to find tickets somewhere. No luck.

Then I got a call from a local car dealer in Las Vegas. Larry Carter was a GM dealer. He called me and said these exact words. "Hey Simon, I have these tickets to some soccer event in Los Angeles. I don't like soccer. You want em?" I asked him politely what they were and he said they were for the World Cup Final or something.

I'm really lucky I didn't get a speeding ticket on the way to his dealership.

One of the highlights of my life was sitting with my Dad in the Rose Bowl among more than 100,000 people as Brazil beat Italy on penalty kicks. The game itself was a bit of a snoozer, but the atmosphere was electric.

More important, the chance to host the World Cup led to the creation of Major League Soccer, North America's premier league. Not all markets can or will be successful, but I look at the MLS as an adolescent trying to find himself. Trying to market soccer like baseball or basketball won't work. It is not the same. Soccer fans are different. We didn't have the advantage of growing up watching our heroes on TV, like baseball or basketball.

Our heroes were either local guys or, once every four years, we got to see the World Cup. Occasionally, we saw a game from Germany or some other faraway locale, but it wasn't the same. Soccer in the country has to be marketed differently. It has to appeal to the fan who played as a kid while still trying to reach a mass market. This has proved to be very, very difficult.

The one stroke of genius was bringing in David Beckham because of his worldwide appeal. Here was this handsome guy who was a true star and now was in Los Angeles. That got attention. MLS got a huge boost. The casual U.S. sports fan took notice of soccer a little more. This was coupled with the U.S. National team playing so well in the 2006 World Cup. At that point, the MLS was 10 years old and made the bold move to get Beckham. While the serious soccer fan understands that Beckham isn't going to score goal after goal, he created a buzz.

Soon after that, people who knew nothing about soccer were talking to me about it. Lots of them were clueless, but it didn't matter. They were talking about it. I found myself waking up early in 2010 to watch the World Cup. The difference is that instead of sitting at home at 5 in the morning and feeling slightly embarrassed to be one of the few guys watching it, I was at the Fireside Tavern in Las Vegas - owned by my friend Coby Holt -with hundreds of my newly soccer-crazed friends. People who didn't know Zinedine Zidane from Baked Ziti were asking me if head-butting was legal. Not that it mattered, all that mattered was that they were into it.

Soccer had finally arrived and this time it was different than the NASL. This time around it looks sustainable.

One look at the Pacific Northwest will validate the game to most. Take in a game in Vancouver, Seattle or Portland and you will begin to understand the game that I grew up around. The passion is palpable and this is happening in other cities like Kansas City, Salt Lake and New York. But, for me, these Pacific Northwest rivalries reminded me of my youth and the game I grew to love. Now, my friends Mallett and Nash are actual owners of the Vancouver Whitecaps. How cool is that?

The MLS will spawn a new generation of players. At 15, my son Sean could maybe be one of them someday. I am asked all the time about the youth system in this country and this is my take: The academy system that the U.S. Soccer Federation has, in essence, mandated is an excellent concept.

But there are major issues from my standpoint as a coach, former player and now parent. The academies are supposed to be set up for the elite player. The challenge is defining what an elite player is. With 78 Academies currently operating around the country, there is no way that there are that many "elite" players. Of course, it depends on your definition, but virtually every parent (and player) believes that their child is an elite player or could be.

So the system is set up for everyone to believe they should be in the academy setting. Supply and demand is going to get out of balance and soon there will be "academies" everywhere. This is fine, but as the academy system grows, the very concept of separating elite players from other not-so-elite players will be non-existent. And then another layer will need to be added.

I do believe that higher-level players need to play more. Ten months of the year is appropriate. Playing or practicing four or five days a week is fine, as long as the sessions are managed properly. Just playing is not good enough any more. Short, sharp training sessions are far more effective than long, boring practices. Most of my higher-level sessions in my career, whether they were at the professional or national team level, were short. Maybe an hour to an hour and a half without any time wasted.

This is what many amateur coaches miss. There was always a written plan for practice at the higher levels. Always efficient movement from one drill or exercise to the next and there was never wasted time. We came to work, we did our work and we went home. There was no need to take three hours, but that continues to be a huge problem for amateur coaches in this country.

The other consideration is that new coaches need to understand the role of regeneration, taking days off and what light sessions are compared to tactical sessions or scrimmages. The psychology of players, nutrition, strength and conditioning … these are all very real issues that coaches need to be educated about and have the ability to implement. Sadly there are simply not enough "good" coaches to go around.

But coaching is not the main issue that dissuaded us from sending Sean to an academy. The issue is education and life experience. No matter how good of a player you are, education, and to a lesser extent, the social experience you get in high school are what matters in the end. For our family this was a non-starter when it came to the academy decision. We were not prepared to compromise Sean's education.

If the MLS (and other) academies can build a system where the players are also working in an elite educational setting, then I think things will change for us. Until then, we determined that it was not worth the risk to compromise Sean's education.

In Canada, we grew upon on the Major Junior Hockey system, which reminds me a lot of the academy system for soccer. Kids moved away from home as early as 14, where they lived either together or with a family, and they focused on hockey. Although some made it, including some of my friends like Russ and Geoff Courtnall, many, many more did not.

Sadly, too many people base the evaluation of the program on the successful people. The guys who make it get all the kudos and the people who run the program point out those guys. This is simply not reality. For every Russ Courtnall, there are dozens, maybe hundreds of guys who did not make it. The academy system for soccer will work the same way. These kids will move away from home, live, eat, sleep and breathe the game, and then get tossed out when they are not good enough.

That is devastating and until the academy program includes a strong educational component that gives these kids a strong chance for success when they fail in soccer, it's not a program I can feel comfortable putting my son in or endorsing. If he is good enough after high school, then that is a different story. But for now, he is staying put at his awesome school – Bishop Gorman High School – and will develop his game in the traditional system.

I realize this is just our opinion and our decision. I don't judge others for committing to academies. I hope their kids have a great experience and that it all works out. I'm just concerned because I realize how easily the dream can come and go. Every kid should dream of making it in the game. Each kid, no matter where they fit on their current team has a chance.

That is the beauty of this game. You don't have to be physically imposing, or the fastest player, or the strongest. I look back at my upbringing and know for a fact that I was the third best child in my house and, for a long time, not nearly as good as my dad. Heck, my mom and the family dog might have given me a run for my money at times. I know that on many of the teams I played on, I was probably near the bottom of the list. Absolutely no one would have guessed that I would have made it professionally.

And certainly no one would ever have thought I would make it with someone else's heart. The game is beautiful, full of passion, hope, love and despair. It will bring you lifelong friends and incredible memories.

It will deliver some of the best experiences of your life and it will break your heart.

But even that you can recover from. I know. I did it.

6

Victoria Kicks In

I come by my love of soccer honestly. Between my father's background, my brothers' ability, my competitiveness with them and everything else, I was born to play the game, even if I didn't ever expect to one day go pro. When I was younger, I played all sorts of sports. In the neighborhood where I grew up, there were about 60 kids and we played everything all the time. There would always be kids at our house. It was like my mom was constantly cooking and feeding everybody. Sometimes there would be 18 guys at the house and nine times out of 10 it was the soccer guys. It was great.

I always came back to soccer. The game was perfect for my size. Basketball was out by high school and baseball wasn't my thing. The turning point, as I mentioned, was the British Columbia tournament I played in as a junior in high school. I was at Mount Douglas High School. My brother Marc played for Oak Bay High and Adam spent one year at Victoria High before we moved into the Mount Doug district. It was probably just coincidence that their soccer team was going to be the best in the city for the next few years. After that high school tournament and my experience on the National Youth team, the recognition was starting to get more serious. I graduated in 1983 and faced the first of some interesting choices.

I was 18 at the time and decided to go to England to play for the Millwall Football Club in London. Millwall was known as the Lions and, at the time, played in the third division of English Soccer. Millwall moved up to the second division the next season. Just as now, teams could be promoted or relegated to leagues from year to year depending on how they performed. The goal, of course, was to play in the First Division, what they call the Barclays Premier League now (that was the name they came up with in 1992).

Back then, Millwall was working its way up. By the time I got there, the team was playing its 99th season. Talk about tradition, this was amazing stuff. Millwall had been formed by a bunch of workers from the J.T. Morton's canning and preserve factory in Millwall, which is part of London's East End. The team was known as the Dockers then, a tribute to the fact many of its supporters worked at the Millwall Dock. This was a working-class team of working-class men in one of the poorest, toughest areas of London. It was team for tough guys and tough fans. One of the first places it played games was in a field behind The Lord Nelson pub on a little patch of land known as the Isle of Dogs.

The team migrated from the East End to the southeast part of London, but the change didn't mean much to the type of people who followed the team. In the 1970s and 1980s, Millwall became famous – or infamous, if you prefer– for the hooligans who followed the team. A gang known as the Millwall Bushwackers was the most famous (years later, they would serve as the antagonists in the 2005 film *Green Street Hooligans)*. That was back when fan violence in soccer really peaked. The club was fined time and again for crowd violence and the ruling body of English soccer actually shut down matches on five occasions.

In 1977, only six years before I got there, the people who ran Millwall invited the British Broadcasting Company's documentary program Panorama to do a show on the fans. Club officials maintained that the hooligan reputation was blown out of proportion by the media. The whole thing backfired when the BBC instead did a show on how deeply rooted hooliganism was with Millwall, even linking the club with the far-right political party the National Front.

Again, that's just the way it was with Millwall. Back in the early 1900s, Millwall used to play matches against rival clubs made up of other workers from businesses that competed with Millwall businesses. It was basically like a free-for-all of workers fighting it out not just for a soccer game, but for their working lives. Think about how brutal that must have been. We're talking about people really playing for keeps. The history of the club being shut down for violence dated to the 1920s, when opposing players and referees would be attacked from time to time.

When I got there, they still told stories about the 1960s, when Millwall had a streak of 59 straight matches without a loss. When the streak finally ended in 1967, the fans broke all the windows in the opposing team's bus. Then, in 1978, during an FA Cup game against Ipswich, a riot broke out in the stands after Ispwich took a 6-1 lead. After the game, the manager of Ipswich famously said of the Millwall hooligans, "(The police) should have turned the flamethrowers on them."

So I walked into all of this in September 1983, just months after graduating from high school. It was awesome. I wanted to play for the best soccer teams in the world, which I thought were in England, of course. To me, you might as well test yourself against the best, that's how I looked at it. Let me say that in the third division, it was tough, fast paced, soccer that took some time to get used to. At the time, I stayed with my uncle, Malcolm Keith (my dad's brother), and his wife Laurette.

Everything about playing in Millwall was fantastic. The level of play, the enthusiasm for the game, my teammates, the whole thing. You couldn't ask for a better environment to become a better player. I was there nearly a year and I grew more as player than at any other time in my career. I lived like a monk. My days were all the same. Up at 7 a.m., have bowl of cereal and two pieces of toast for breakfast. Then I'd catch the bus (Malcolm eventually gave me a car, which added to the adventure) to get to the training ground in Eltham for a 9 a.m. start. Training went from 9 to 11:30.

Take a shower, get dressed and then grab two ham-and-cheese buns and a cup a tea from the tea lady in the on-site "club house," which was really nothing more than a glorified gardener's shack. I would sometimes go hang out with a friend from Victoria, Neil Ryan, who was living with relatives in Eltham at the time. Then it was back to training in the afternoon or, if there was no training, back to Bromley (where Malcolm and Laurette lived) to lift weights at the local club. I would return to their house by about 4:30 and eat a GIGANTIC meal. I would eat anything and everything I could get my hands on. Then I'd watch a little TV at night and be in bed by 9 p.m.

Games would be on Saturday with Sundays off and then back to the same routine on Monday. I did this literally every day for close to a year. This wasn't some sight-seeing experience. The only thing I did for recreation was go see Adam occasionally. He was living in Reading, a three-hour train ride away. Neil would come along and we'd have a good time, but when I say it was occasional, I truly mean that. Make no mistakes, I was there to play. And play I did. This was the beginning of my ability to really put blinders on and focus on one task relentlessly.

I had two very vivid memories of my time in England this time around. One was soccer related. One not so much.

The daily grind of training at Millwall was simply awesome for me. I loved it. I was playing in the reserves and playing in the very competitive combination league. This was a league made up of all teams from around the south including every London side. The big clubs used the reserves for a place for first-teamers to get their feet under them if they were coming back from injury or not getting enough time in the first team for whatever reason. The level was very, very good. On any given day you would play against excellent players and frequently you would match up against truly great ones. It was on one of these days that provided me the highlight of my year as it relates to the field.

It was the middle of February. I had been at Millwall since August and the players were beginning to trust me. I was becoming a regular in the team. We had a mid-week game against Arsenal at Highbury. As a young kid I was a Gunners fan – ever so briefly before changing my allegiance to Brian Clough and Nottingham Forest, but that is a different story. So off to Highbury we go, to play one of the great teams in the world in one of the most historic stadiums.

None of that meant much to me…until I got in the locker room.

First, the locker room was huge. Bigger than any locker room I had ever been in. Second, it was all marble. Marble floors, marble ceilings, marble benches, marble baths, marble, marble, marble. This was elegant. So as I began to undress, I was dreading putting my feet on the cold marble. It was February so it was still cold and any soccer player will tell you they never, ever want to start the game with cold feet. Well, as I take my sock off and put my foot down, the floor is warm. I couldn't believe it. The benches were warm too. All the marble in the dressing room at Highbury was heated from below. Now I know that it doesn't seem very impressive now but to a teenage kid wet behind the ears from little, far away Victoria, B.C., it was that "Welcome to the big time" moment.

And that wasn't even the highlight of the day.

Lining up for Arsenal that day were the gigantic and imposing England central defensive pair of Tony Adams and Martin Keown. Both were star players and full experienced Internationals, at the top of their game. To top off the challenge, behind them was current England goalie Jon Lucic. For Millwall playing up front against them was Teddy Sherringham, a big strapping lad at the time who went on to an incredible career with Tottenham, Manchester United and England, to name a few. He was also one of the nicest guys I have met in the game.

And then there's me at all of 5-foot-8, 165 pounds and still thinking about the warm marble in the locker room.

Little Millwall was able to steal a result that day from Arsenal and I was in the middle of it. In about the 65th minute, as I am sure both Adams and Keown were marking the imposing Sherringham, I was able to sneak in behind them and slot the ball between the legs of the on-rushing Lucic for the only goal of the match. I have scored lots of goals in my career (although many coaches will say not enough), but none is burned into my memory like that one. Think about hitting a home run at Yankee Stadium or scoring a touchdown at Lambeau Field. This was THAT moment for me. It was really cool and I replay it in my head from time to time. It was so beautiful, especially since we won the game.

Driving back on the bus that day with the guys, Sherringham made a point of coming up to me and trying to put it into perspective. "We won 1-nil and you scored at Arsenal. Do you realize that! You scored at Arsenal." Teddy may not even remember me let alone the game or the goal or the trip, but that was the kind of guy he was. He had a way of making a "lesser" teammate like me feel welcome and appreciated. I am not surprised that he became one of the great English players of his time.

The next vivid memory of England might not be as glamorous but it gives another peak into this most valuable time. As I have said, I really lived like a monk in England. Head down, focused on being the very best I could be. Adam was training in Reading, west of London and a bit difficult to get to from where I was. Adam made the trip to me more often than I did to him.

One weekend, I made the trip to visit him. He had a great friend, Neville Johns, who played and was born in Reading. Johns was a very good player, but enjoyed the fun side of life. Much like Adam, Johns just wasn't much for the grind of daily training.

Upon arrival at 11 a.m., we headed straight to the pub. Being raised in Reading, Johns was very well known and very well liked. We spent many, many hours in the pub, just laughing and being lads, as they say. Well, by 4 p.m., I was hammered. We made a quick stop at his mom's to go get changed and off we went to the club. Problem was I was actually a bit more than hammered. I hadn't been drinking any alcohol at all for the past six months or so and it hit me like a free kick to the stones. Walking to the next club was just too much. As we passed a TESCO (a grocery store chain in England), I noticed a shopping cart. In I jumped. Adam and Neville had to push me to the bar in a shopping cart. I was able to sober up a bit and we enjoyed ourselves at the bar. We eventually made our way back home, although I'm not sure if it was really late at night or early in the morning. As we rounded the corner we ran into about eight white guys who all had these shaved heads and looked like they wanted some trouble. Maybe they were what used to be known as "skinheads," but I'm not completely sure. All I know is that one of them called out Johns, who is black. Immediately I sobered up and I knew this was going to be trouble.

Before I knew it, Adam had been hit by this one guy who was on crutches. The guy blindsided Adam with a crutch to the face. There was blood everywhere. Now it was on. The next 30 seconds would be freaking hilarious if not for how terrifying it was. All of the skinheads wanted a piece of Johns. He had seen this before, living in a still racially volatile country, and knew exactly what he needed to do. I thought it was run.

Nope.

As one of the skinheads made a charge at Johns, I remember this as if it was in slow motion. With one punch, Johns connected right on the button. I am sure this dude's nose was broken, but no one knew because with that one punch that dude hit the floor like a bag of bricks. He was out cold. The other seven kind of looked at each other and decided they would take their anger elsewhere. They picked up their friend and went on their way with their tails between their legs.

It was incredible. I didn't do a thing and all of a sudden I felt totally bad ass. But it taught me an important lesson about being a high profile person – Johns not me.

I stayed at Millwall for almost a year before I got an offer to play for the Canadian National Program at the University of Victoria. I made the decision to return home and attempt to play for the Canadian World Cup team. In hindsight, I probably should have stayed in England.

The problem with staying in England was more that it was just tough mentally. By May 1984, I was turning 19 and for some reason I made the easy choice. I was tired. I was just so homesick. Maybe I knew deep down I needed to be home.

Eventually I went back to England in 1989 after my heart surgery and played for another six months. I did the semi-pro thing that time around, which was cool and the players were great to me. But I was a lot older by then. I was pretty much a man that time. In my first trip, I was really still a kid in a lot of ways.

There were some other benefits to me playing in England. First, it created quite a buzz back home that made me better known around Victoria. Here was some guy straight out of high school going to England to pursue a soccer career. That was pretty interesting. Why that mattered didn't have anything to do with my ego. Rather, it was about people just knowing that I was somebody to root for. I was somebody they were interested in and that helped when it came to fundraising later on.

Second, it allowed me to renew my British citizenship, which became crucial when I had to go to England for a transplant. Yes, I was still technically a British citizen since I was born there, but this made it easier to sell to the people there later. Did it ultimately matter? I'm not sure, but I needed every bit of help I could get.

When I came back to Canada, I enrolled at the University of Victoria and started playing in the Canadian National Program. By this time, a lot of people were starting to think about Canada making the World Cup tournament in 1986 and that bug got in my ear. I realized pretty fast that the caliber of soccer I was playing wasn't nearly as good as in England, but I had made my decision and now I was focused on playing in the World Cup. I had a real chance to play for my country on soccer's biggest stage. I had been selected by the program to live and train full-time with the National Program, go to college and live in my hometown. It was a pretty good deal.

At the University of Victoria, I played for both the National Program with different coaches coming in and out of the program and for Bruce Twamley with the university team. Twamley was a really good former player who had been born in Victoria, one of the best to come out of this soccer-rich community. He was in his mid-30s by then, but had been quite a player in his prime. In the 1970s, he had gone to play in England for Ipswich Town, but he returned to play in the North American Soccer League. He then played for the New York Cosmos for a brief time, Minnesota, Oakland and Edmonton before ending up back at UVic. Twamley seemed to have paid his dues, so I was looking forward to playing for him.

So from July 1985 through late in the year, I was doing fine, training, playing and taking classes. Around November I played in a tournament in Regina. That was in the middle of the country, "the prairies" as we like to call them. Ironically, Regina is only a couple of hours from Lestock where we lived briefly before settling in Victoria. During that trip, I got sick. You think it's just normal, a sniffle, some congestion, the typical stuff you fight through when you're young and playing for a team. My parents thought it might be the flu, but I didn't think twice about it.

I had been enjoying being home after a year of living like a monk. I had reconnected with some old friends and made some new ones. Our crew of Brad McAdams, Clay Crust, Wade Loukes, along with some of our other teammates, were certainly enjoying our time as young athletes in a sports mad city. But, as I said before, this pesky flu didn't really go away. For a while, I thought it might be mononucleosis, but that was obviously wrong. After a few months of that, my mom and dad started sending me to specialists. The first one was the "idiot" that thought it was stress.

Next, we got to some doctors who thought I had something called Raynaud's disease. While that can also be related to stress, it was closer to what was actually happening. Raynaud's disease – or "phenomenon" as it's sometimes called – is another circulatory issue where your hands can get discolored. That was another one that eventually got dismissed when the doctor figured out I was suffering from some kind of virus. Later, I got to a cardiologist who diagnosed me with myocarditis and he thought we had caught it early enough.

The problem with that is that it can be like 30 different viruses, so the doctors kept bringing me back and forth to the hospital to figure out which one it could be. Then they'd give me some kind of medicine to deal with it, and as soon as I took it, I felt great and went right back to training. I'd want to play tennis or workout or just do something. I kept thinking that what was wrong with me was going to get solved and I would be fine. I also started taking prednisone for the first time and, of course, that really helped me start to feel better. Being on steroids like that completely covered the fact that my heart function was deteriorating at a pretty quick pace.

While this was going on, my hopes of making the national team were growing. I was sure I was going to be part of that historic team. This was really exciting stuff for me, and I was actually playing pretty well despite my condition. Obviously, the medication was getting me through it, and as soon as I went off the medication, I would get worse.

That's what led to me and Twamley getting into that big argument at the end of 1985 and him suspending me. I was really upset with him telling me I wasn't being a team player. I yelled back at him that he was making that up. As it turned out, he was absolutely right with his analysis of me. He is a good man and a good soccer man. He got the short end of my temper and my frustrations. I have talked to him since then about this part of my life. It was just a crappy deal all the way around. It was bad for me because my health sucked and it was bad for him because he had to deal with something he hadn't really been told about. It was also bad for the team because they saw only a shell of me.

But at the time, I was pissed.

It was shortly after Twamley suspended me that my mother saw how white my hands and feet had become and she really started pushing for better care. It was also at about this time when the people around Victoria started to help in a huge way. By October 1985, it was obvious I was getting very sick. Family friend Cheryl Clark, and some people from the Victoria Youth Soccer Association, such as Eric Bonham and Pat Burns, approached me and my family about starting the Simon Keith Fund. They asked us whether we would accept the money if they raised it.

The community fund took off once the Victoria Police Department jumped in. I didn't know a lot about the finances, but I knew the money issues were already getting to be hard on my folks. Beyond that group of people, we had so many friends who helped, like the McAdams Family. Bette, the mom, helped take care of me a lot of the time when I was still in Victoria.

Bette McAdams is one of those rare people in this world who is just good. She came into my life at the exact moment I needed her and gave me exactly what I needed when I needed it. I had met Brad McAdams a few years earlier in high school, although we weren't really close then. Brad was a year younger than me, so when I got back from England we played on the same summer team. Once we were at UVIC, we became very good friends because we were now in the same class. We would spend hours and hours over at his house, causing the usual trouble that college kids get into. Most of it not printable!

I became friendly with the whole family. When I got sick and was in the hospital doing tests for a day and then later a few days and later a few weeks at a time, Bette would drop in. First, it was occasionally. She would just drop in a say hello and stay a few minutes to make sure I was OK. As time went on and my hospital stays were longer and more frequent, Bette showed up more and more. She would bring me little things, like candy, a card or some chocolate milk. It got to the point that she came every day and sat with me and played cards. It also got to a point that I needed her to come. We would play cribbage for hours and hours on end. My mom and dad had been dealing with all the tough stuff, but Bette provided a place for me to feel safe. I could say anything to her and I knew it would be OK. She was an angel sent to me.

Obviously, the healthcare itself was covered by the British Columbia health plan. That's part of Canada's form of socialized medicine. The issue of socialized healthcare is an enormous one in the United States, with lots of debate about it still going on as I write this in 2012. But the system was a life-saver for my family financially. Still, this wasn't a cheap proposition and what the people did in Victoria was amazing.

The problem financially was the constant travel to Vancouver to see the doctors I needed to see. Sometimes we'd be gone for days at a time, so there were hotel costs on top of taking the ferry all the time. It wasn't a lot at any one time, but it added up fast as I went to the doctors again and again. At the time, my parents were already talking about selling the house to pay for a lot of the cost, so this was a big relief. The Victoria police kicked in the first $1,000 and offered to set up the station as a dropoff point for more donations. That worked out great because it made the whole fund seem much more legitimate.

As an aside, in the years since I went through all of this, The David Foster Foundation (davidfosterfoundation.com) was started to assist families just like mine who are thrust into this predicament. David Foster, the world-renowned musician, is from Victoria and has a great story about how his foundation started. He has gone on to become one of the great philanthropists of his time in Canada, assisting families with these types of expenses when they have a child in need of an organ transplant. When you are faced with the decision to save your child's life or pay the power bill, it is no contest. The problem is that this is not a fairy tale and the power bill still needs to get paid.

A lot of the reason that I got support and attention was people started to realize how good a soccer player I was. From my 11th grade year in high school in 1982, to now, my profile was getting bigger and bigger. I had been on the National Youth Team, so I had a little celebrity from soccer. In addition, both of my brothers had helped build the family name in terms of on-field success. Throw in the fact that Canada was finally going to play in the World Cup and interest in soccer was at an all-time high. All of that helped me.

More important, I think my father was a huge trigger for all of this. By the time I got sick, he had been in Victoria as a teacher for more than 15 years. And when you're a P.E. teacher, you touch a lot of lives and do it primarily in a positive way. For instance, the Victoria Police Department was really helpful because my dad had been such a help to them for years and years. The VPD used to run a basketball tournament every year and it was hosted by Central Junior High, where my dad was the P.E. teacher and ran the athletic program. I even played in the tournament one year. My dad was the point man at the school for anything the police needed to get things done and host the tournament.

He didn't do it for money. He did it because he believed that sports were the best way to keep kids out of trouble and to teach them the necessary lessons to succeed in life. If my dad had a nickel for every kid who said to me, "Man I hated your Dad when I went to Central, but now I realize what he was doing and he is by far my favorite teacher of all time and he had such an impact in my life," he would be a very rich man. I actually chuckle every time

I bump into anyone who was taught by my dad. Literally everyone feels the same way and there is no greater compliment a teacher can get.

Again he never did what he did for money and the police understood that, which is why they endorsed the fund. That was a huge relationship for my family to have.

The other thing is that my dad had actually coached one of the policemen who helped us out the most. That's what being part of a community is about. My dad didn't ask for anything back for the 40 years he gave to community. He did everything because he thought it was the right thing to do. But when I was in deep trouble – and by extension he was – the community didn't need to be asked. What a cool legacy.

After the family and police got the fund kick started, everybody seemed to do something. There were benefit dances and a match between the Canadian national team (the squad I was supposed to join one day) and the Vancouver Island League selects. Then, in the biggest stunner, there was an anonymous donation of $10,000 through the Dream Maker's program.

The most touching moment was when this 7-year-old boy who I had coached decided he didn't want presents for his birthday. Instead, he asked for donations to help me. I mean, that's the kind of stuff that makes you hold your breath for a second to fight back the tears. We gave the boy a blown up picture of me with my autograph, but I was too sick to make it to his party. I felt so bad about that.

Tak worked his ass off to raise money, collecting $7,000 himself. When you have people fighting for you like that, it helps build a positive state of mind. At one of the dances, people came up to sign a picture of me, putting well wishes on it. As Tak was standing there, one guy looked at my picture and said, "He (looks like he) has maybe 24 hours to live."

There was a downside to the fundraising. In March 1986, after I was told by doctors in Vancouver that I need the transplant and then was told by the doctors in Ontario that I didn't, the money became an issue. People didn't understand that I still actually needed the transplant at some point, but maybe not as early as expected. I had to come back from Ontario and put a good face on the whole thing. But that was after we spent $5,000 out of the $30,000 for plane tickets and lodging when we were in Ontario.

After we got back and got done holding another press conference of answering questions, my father got a phone call from a man with the Dream Makers Foundation.

The man asked my dad a pretty direct and kind of uncomfortable question.

"I'm wondering what you are going to do with the money now that Simon isn't going to have the transplant?" the man said.

"What do you mean?" my dad replied.

"I mean, what are we supposed to do with the fund?"

"I'd rather not discuss the fund because we haven't even looked into alternatives yet," my dad said.

The money was a blessing, but it was also a bit of a curse at that moment. My dad had to explain publicly the plan for the money -- even though we didn't really have a plan at that point. It's just that uncomfortable situation that crops up when you're dealing with money, especially donated money. Basically, for us to justify getting money, I had to be really sick. I was, but the people of Ontario didn't agree, and that put us in a bad situation for a couple of weeks.

As it turned out, we needed at least that much money for what was to come.

7

THE ENGLISH PATIENCE

My personal savior nearly gave up a future in medicine to become a Hungarian Freedom Fighter.

All I can say is, thank God the woman Sir Terence English was dating at the time talked some sense into him.

English is the father of Britain's heart transplant programs. While he doesn't quite rank with the likes of Dr. Norman Shumway, Dr. Richard Lower or Dr. Christiaan Barnard in terms of breakthroughs at the genesis of heart transplant surgery, he fought through the politics of morality in England to create the program that ultimately saved my life. He is also the person who approved me for surgery. My debt to him is as great as it is to anyone.

But I was lucky in a way because English was a little different than all of them. He was brave in a way that went beyond medical science. That's what allowed him to push against the social and political pressure that was initially against heart transplant procedures in England. His story is one of amazing focus and perseverance.

In 1956, English was a 24-year-old medical student at Guy's College, a medical school in London that was part of Guy's Hospital. English was also a trained mining engineer by that time, having learned the trade in South Africa, drilling for diamonds in Rhodesia and then going to Canada for summer jobs over three consecutive years. (Ironically my future in-laws came from South Africa and Rhodesia).

Toward the end of his first year in medical school, English was, in American parlance, "burned out." He was unsure if he wanted to keep training to be a doctor, go back to mining or, for a fleeting moment, become a Hungarian Freedom Fighter when the country revolted against its communist government.

Fortunately, English's romance with a 30-year-old woman kept him from joining the bloody fray. She talked some sense into him, or so he said in his autobiography, *Follow Your Star*.

For the next year, English was undecided about his future. Little did he know, the future of heart transplant surgery in England rested on his decision. Little did he know, my life depended on his decision.

English was still in medical school, but his spirit wasn't there. Or as he put it in his book: "When I arrived back in England I had just turned twenty-four and the next year proved to be the most turbulent and difficult of my life...As the days passed I grew more and more dissatisfied with my lot and depressed at the thought of what lay ahead. And in this state of turmoil I went to see the Dean and told him that I wanted to give up medicine. He observed that I was old enough to know my own mind and that was that. It all had a rather dreamlike quality about it as I had no clear thought as to what path my future should take."

At that time, English wanted to leave London altogether. The only thing that kept him there was a promise to his mother to stay until his sister got married. Even then, there were moments when he considered bolting, such as when the when the Hungarian Revolution started in October. He wanted to be a "freedom fighter," but the woman he was seeing talked him out of it. In the spring of 1957, after his sister got married, he took a job with a company called Kennco and went on a mining expedition in the Ungava Peninsula in Canada. That area of Canada is about as desolate as it gets, treeless tundra populated by Eskimos (or Inuit Indians, as they are also known) – a tough people. It's at the north end of the Quebec Province. English started off the journey by staying in Quebec City, but then spent July and August at a campsite, mapping the area, studying the geology, watching the geese migrate south (the first signs of winter start in August in this part of the world), listening to the loons and hoping for a brisk wind to keep the "ubiquitous mosquitoes" at bay.

Perhaps the idea of making this his life's work, or just the chance to be away from school for a few months, gave English the time to refocus on what he wanted to do. As he wrote: "I think the new environment and the ability to discuss thoughts ... helped to crystallise (sic) the view that I had made a serious mistake in giving up medicine." After that, English wrote a letter to the Dean at Guy's, Dr. George Houston, politely begging to be re-admitted to the medical school. I'm not much for long-winded talking or writing, but the letter is perfect in tone and manner.

Dear Sir:

Last October, shortly after starting my second year at Guy's, I decided to give up my medical studies and at an interview with you on 17ᵗʰ October I informed you of my decision. I told myself then that I no longer wanted to be a doctor and that it would be wiser for me to continue with the profession that I was already qualified in.

Looking back on it I can see that apart from being in an unsettled state of mind my action was predominantly a result of impatience and weakness. On the one had I could see year of hard study ahead; on the other a job which already offered substantial financial rewards.

Soon after leaving I began to apprehend the full meaning of my loss and on occasions I came close to asking for re-admittance to the School. But then I also felt that I had made my decision and that I could not expect other than to remain with it. However, as the days go by I realise (sic) ever more strongly that it is medicine that I want to do. This decision, born during my third year at University in South Africa, has I think always been with me. But previously I would not recognise (sic) the fact that anything worthwhile in life could not, of necessity, be achieved with ease.

So I write now and ask you to consider my case compassionately. I realise (sic) that my conduct so far has not been such as to warrant a sympathetic reaction, but I do ask you to give serious consideration to my plea. On my part, all I can offer is the assurance that, if given the opportunity of recommencing my studies at Guy's, I would do everything in my power to be worthy of the trust shown.

I know that it will require discipline and industry and that it will involve certain sacrifices. But I feel sincerely that my desire to be a doctor is now mature and strong enough to enable me to achieve the goal. I ask you to have faith in this.

Yours faithfully,

Terence English

Fortunately for English, (and the yet-to-be-born me), Houston and the people in charge at Guy's gave him a second chance. Just as fortunately, Dr. English is someone whose life very much mirrors my father's, complete with an understated toughness and resolve. Maybe that's because both of them lost their fathers at an early age. English's father died of respiratory failure when he was only 18 months old. His father was a trained mining engineer and the family lived in South Africa, although they had strong roots in England as well.

Arthur English had also been a war hero, a decorated pilot from World War I who survived being shot in the stomach and shot down from the skies. Sadly, between being gassed in the war and breathing the heavy dust of the gold mines of South Africa and Rhodesia, Arthur English's body gave out on him at 49. Still, brave men like that endure in the consciousness of a son.

Maybe that's why English was willing to take a chance on returning to medical school. Once he did, he threw himself into his studies. By 1963, English was working in the Thoracic Unit at Guy's Hospital. That year, while vacationing in South Africa, English had two life-altering encounters. First, he met his first wife, Ann. Second, he met Barnard and observed him in surgery. It was a purely chance meeting and Barnard was still four years from performing the world's first heart transplant in December 1967, but it was important nonetheless. In some way, it helped stoke English's passion and understanding about the how to conduct his eventual program. As unimpressed as English was with Barnard's technical skill and behavior (Barnard was very harsh with his staff during surgery), English took great note of Barnard's attention to detail.

Over the next 10 years, English was increasingly drawn down the path of heart transplantation. He worked at the London Chest Hospital and did a yearlong research fellowship in the United States. He eventually moved to Papworth Hospital in 1972 and worked with fellow cardiothoracic surgeon Ben Milstein. In early 1973, he took a two-week leave to go back to the United States to meet with surgeons at Stanford University and the Mayo Clinic to observe how their heart transplant programs were progressing. Shumway's program at Stanford had done much of the work developing protocols for heart transplant surgeries, such as the surgical techniques and studying the phenomenon of organ rejection. The fact that Barnard beat Shumway to the first heart transplant didn't take away from the feeling in the medical community that Shumway was really the expert.

English worked with Dr. Philip Caves, Shumway's protégé at Stanford, and, more important, observed what was going on with the early heart-transplant patients. According to English, of the first patients to receive heart transplants from 1967 to 1970, just over half lived beyond one month, and only a very few made it more than two years. In England, the results were similarly bad. English's mentor, Dr. Donald Ross, performed three heart surgeries during that time. The patients lived, respectively, 45, two, and 107 days. Thus, around the same time English was visiting Stanford and the Mayo Clinic, England basically declared a moratorium on heart transplants. Sir George Godber, the Chief Medical Officer for Health, declared in January 1973 that there would be no support for any further attempts.

Fortunately, English said he was "unaware" of the moratorium. Maybe he just subconsciously ignored it. Either way, by the time he got to Stanford in early 1973, Shumway's group had made improvements in the program. The results were getting more encouraging. Cave had come up with a procedure that helped detect possible rejection earlier and survival rates were growing. By late 1973, English returned to Papworth and was convinced it was time to open a heart transplant center in England.

His immediate colleagues weren't. The two cardiologists at Papworth, Hugh Fleming and David Evans, were either "neutral" (Fleming) or "expressed strong opposition based on clinical, ethical and religious grounds" (Evans). As English wrote of Evans in his biography: "During all the years that followed, he remained highly critical of the work and could never accept the diagnosis of brain death, thereby leading him to accuse me on a number of occasions of removing hearts from people who were still alive."

In 2011, English reflected on the situation during my trip to England: "It was quite the political and moral battle. You would attempt to have a logical conversation about something you felt most doctors would be interested in promoting. We were trying to advance medicine and I felt most people understood that, but you had certain people holding us back, really battling against the things I wanted to do. I understood some of them who had a moral objection. That was their belief system. But others were doing it because they felt purely that if people were suddenly against organ donation that their business might be affected. It was annoying, to say the least."

Actually asking for hearts wasn't a much easier task, as English explained years later.

"You had to measure the situation when you approached a donor family. Some of them were simple. The family was either very generous or indifferent to the idea of donating organs, which made the situation easier. They were either happy to know that people would be helped or weren't interested in what was going to happen," English said. "But there would be others where the grief had hit them in such a difficult fashion that it was too hard to imagine. One time, I happened upon a couple who had just lost a relatively young daughter to a horse riding accident. I asked them if they were willing to donate and they couldn't imagine giving up any of her.

"In some respects, you're looking at them and thinking, 'You have a chance to give life to someone else, to save someone,' but you can't say that out loud. I would listen, smile, thank them for their time and then leave. There was no trying to convince them. That's one of the reasons I was so annoyed when other doctors would talk about me violating some code of morality. I was never going to pressure anyone, even if I knew how desperately someone might need that heart. You simply couldn't cross that line."

The line that did have to be crossed was a moral-intellectual divide over what comprised "brain death." Rather that sustaining someone's life indefinitely, English pushed for there to be a definition of when the brain was dead, even if the heart and other organs might still be functioning. For doctors such as Evans, this created an endless argument over what they considered ethical. This kind of discussion never really occurred with kidney patients because those in need of a kidney could continue on dialysis machines. Doctors looking to harvest kidneys were in no rush and could wait for a donor to suffer complete death. No such long-term care machines were in place for those needing heart transplants.

Getting to that argument took more than two years. English spent much of that time doing practical preparations, such as putting together an adequate staff and going through surgical procedures with that staff on open-heart patients, approximating the steps and protocols for a heart transplant. By the middle of 1976, English had a team in place and the group was doing test runs with pig heart transplants. Finally, the Chief Medical Officer of England came up with a definition that somewhat defined brain death. Even then, progress continued to be slow. It wasn't until February 1977 that England's Department of Health "defined the criteria that would have to be met by any centre wishing to embark on heart transplant," English wrote.

By 1978, infighting between English and another surgeon, Dr. Roy Calne, slowed the cooperation between hospitals needed to get the heart transplant program started. It wasn't until early January 1979, when the British Medical Journal ran an extensive article about Shumway's improved success at Stanford, that momentum started to build. On Jan. 14, 1979 (and with Calne out of the country), English and his group finally received news that a heart was available. More than five years of waiting was coming to an end.

As English wrote in his biography: "This was the breakthrough we had been waiting for. The size of the heart and the blood group were suitable for one of our potential recipients, a 44-year-old bachelor, Charles McHugh, who had by then spent a prolonged time in Papworth with advanced heart disease and who was now seriously ill. Having obtained his agreement and spoken to his sister who was a nursing sister in Surrey, we made plans to go ahead with the operation that evening. I had previously decided that I should do both the donor and the transplant operation as I felt the responsibility of assessing the donor and the suitability of the heart prior to its removal should be mine."

The problem was that in the process of harvesting the donor heart, McHugh's heart also stopped. He was placed on a heart-lung machine, but the problem was that English's team wasn't sure how much brain damage McHugh might have suffered. English made the difficult decision to go on with the operation. While the result was successful at first – the heart worked well in McHugh's body – his brain function had been so damaged that he was never able to recover. He died 17 days after the operation. The death, like the ones before it in England, created a hostile political environment for English. Just 10 days after McHugh's death, English had to speak in front of the Transplant Advisory Panel. Although there was such vocal support, the panel refused to help with funding for the program.

In March 1979, a little more than a month after that meeting, the political in-fighting continued. English informed Calne that another potential heart recipient had been accepted to the Papworth program. English asked Calne if, while Calne was away for four weeks, it would be all right to seek heart donors. Calne responded that he and his colleagues "remained very worried at the effect that requesting for heart donation may have on our kidney donations and that therefore unless the relative of a potential donor specifically request that the heart be used for transplantation, we should not be involved in trying to get hearts." Calne's continued the tug-of-war later by making it a rule that his group wouldn't harvest kidneys from donors who agreed to give up their hearts. The fight became almost childish.

But on August 18, 1979, came the biggest and most important breakthrough for English. This was nearly six years after he had started pushing for the program and just seven years before I was going to become one of his patients. With Calne again out of town and unable to interfere, a transplant was arranged for a 52-year-old builder from Wandsworth in London. Keith Castle had been accepted six weeks earlier despite being a heavy smoker with a variety of other minor diseases. But in every other respect, Castle was perfect because he became the face of the heart transplant program in England. As English described: "He had great humour (sic) and fortitude and in every other respect could not have been a better patient. He subsequently became the best possible advertisement for cardiac transplantation, except for his inability to give up smoking … Keith later became somewhat of a national figure as well as an icon for future heart transplant patients. His cockney wit, cheerfulness and enduring optimism, and his gratitude for the extra five-and-a-half years of life granted him, which he put to such good effect, endeared him to everyone he met."

To me, all you need to know about Castle is the "cheerfulness and enduring optimism." He was my kind of guy. This is what I mean by state of mind. So much of the recovery process is about how people approach it. I'll say it time and again, heart transplant surgery isn't easy to recover from. But what do you want to focus on, the hard part, or the part where you get to live longer? If you want to focus on the hard part – the part where you are now a transplant patient – and let that define you, it's only going to hold you back from both getting better and taking advantage of the time you have after the transplant.

After the success with Castle, support started to flow for English. England's National Heart Research Fund provided funding for the next six patients. By 1980, English was getting both government and private support for the program. Eventually, even Calne worked out his problems with English and became part of the heart transplant program. Other cardiovascular surgeons increasingly supported English's work.

As I look at it, the whole thing was so precarious. It took English seven years and a great deal of patience and hard work to get this program up and running. Sure, if English hadn't done this, inevitably someone would have picked up the slack in England and eventually pushed for the heart transplant program. No country as sophisticated as England was going to be left behind when neighboring countries like France were developing programs. Medicine is too competitive a field for that.

But the question for me is whether it would have become good enough fast enough to help me. Here is another example of a person who took a chance on his career. English just as easily could have stayed in mining. Worse, he could have been turned down by the administration at Guy's when he wanted to return. He could have taken the advice of another doctor who told him along the way that he was too old to specialize and that he should have become a general practitioner.

Instead, English took a strong and noble path. He took a chance on his career and did something challenging. Something that, years later, helped save my life.

8

The Journey To Papworth

After I told my friends I'd see them by the end of the summer and boarded the flight from Victoria International Airport to Gatwick Airport in London, I began the most miserable two-plus months of my life and, frankly, my parents' lives. In keeping with that theme, the plane ride itself was a thing of joy. Nine hours and 35 minutes of non-stop flying in a coach seat that isn't meant for human comfort, let alone for someone trying to hold on to their life. Between being too uncomfortable to sleep very long and unable to breathe with much ease, this trip was as miserable as it gets.

I had a window seat on the flight, figuring I would lean against the wall to fall asleep. I miscalculated. The flight took off in mid-afternoon and the sun was bright against the blue sky. The sunshine kept me awake. I put the shade down, but the rest of the passengers on the plane wanted to check the view of the Rocky Mountains, so there was no escaping the light.

By the time I got on that plane, I had been off prednisone for about three weeks and was beginning to find out just how sick I was. I had lost weight and become increasingly pale as my heart continued to degenerate, making it harder and harder to pump blood through my body. Finding a distraction from that discomfort was a constant challenge. I couldn't sleep, the food was awful (but I was hungry), the movie was mediocre and the music was boring. Everything, absolutely everything, was annoying.

When we finally got to London by the next morning, I had plenty of family waiting, from my grandmother and grandfather, Ada and Harry

Simmons, my aunt Eva Goble (my mom's sister) and my favorite uncle Malcolm Keith (my father's brother, who was his usual unpunctual self). When I had played for Millwall in the English League a couple of years before, I lived with Malcolm and his wife Laurette in Bromley, just outside London. They were great, welcoming people whom we had put to the test years before.

Around 1973, my dad had brought a youth soccer team from the Victoria Boys club to England. There were roughly 40 of us on the trip, from kids to coaches to some other parents, but we managed to run out of money on the trip. What do you do when you're out of cash in England? You show up at Malcolm and Laurette's house for sanctuary in their modest home. They completely rolled with the situation. We had people sleeping in every room, including probably a few in the closets. That trip made a huge impression on me about the generosity of family because Malcolm and Laurette came through like troopers.

This time around, the trip was more focused and serious, particularly with my mom with us. She was a picture of anxiety on this trip. She couldn't handle seeing me in pain. On more than one occasion when we were home in Victoria as I was dealing with this, I had glanced up from the dinner table to find her staring at me with that long face. I would bark at her, "What are you looking at?" knowing fully just what she was doing. I understood, but I also needed her to know that I couldn't take the worry. Again, you have to keep focused on the solution, not how you feel about the problem. At times like that, my mother would get up and leave the table. She understood what I needed and that she was too emotional at that moment to give it to me.

At Gatwick, my mother tried to grab my duffel bag when we got to baggage claim. I insisted that she let me carry it. I didn't want to feel like an invalid, even if I couldn't feel comfortable. When we got to Malcolm and Laurette's house, all I wanted to do was lie down on the couch. That was fine, but then I had to deal with people looking at me while my mom tried to catch everybody up on what was happening to me. I couldn't really handle the sorrow. It was all I could do to handle the nausea. I felt like throwing up, which was becoming an increasingly constant part of my life. By a certain point, I felt like I had to throw up every five or 10 minutes. More and more relatives came by as the day went on. There was small talk about the upcoming World Cup, which Canada was about to play in (and which I so desperately wanted to be part of).

That night, exhausted, I slept on the couch. It was the best night of rest I'd had in weeks and probably the best I would have for the next two months or so.

The next day, we went to see Professor John Goodwin, the man I had been sent to see by Dr. Chant back home. We took a cab into London to his office on Cromwell Road, an elegant building with great stone pillars and a series of stairs leading up from the sidewalk. Stairs, just what I needed. My parents had to help me up, which was humiliating. All the while, I kept thinking about whether this was going to be another false hope. Had I traveled some 5,000 miles just to hear more about bureaucracy and politics or, worse, about how my attitude was too blunt? Generally, I'm not a person who gets frustrated, but between my health and the travel, I was getting to that point almost every minute.

In the backdrop of all this was the six-month timeline I had been given by Dr. Ricci in Vancouver in March. Time was ticking away for me, but it was like the way they keep time in a high school soccer match with no scoreboard. There was no clock to watch ticking down the time. You just knew that time was ticking and, in your mind, it was always moving faster than real time, adding to the pressure.

When I finally saw Goodwin, he was impeccably dressed, roughly 5-foot-10 and a thin man. Goodwin, who has since passed away, was in his 70s by then, but still incredibly sharp mentally. He was one of England's – if not one of the world's – leading experts on myocarditis, a man people reached out to even as he had moved into semi-retirement just to pick his brain. We were the latest ones to look to him for help. Goodwin exchanged pleasantries with my parents and me and then tried to pay them a compliment.

"It's remarkable that you would come all this way to help your son," he said. "It's quite a pilgrimage."

My father was direct and abrupt, which probably set a good tone for the meeting.

"I wouldn't call it a pilgrimage," my father said. "We're not desperate. We just want to do whatever needs to be done in order for our son to get better, to get back to normal. It's important that we do something now. The people in Canada would only fight for his life, not the quality of his life. That's why we came here. We couldn't wait around until desperation sets in. No, we're not willing to do that."

I think Goodwin was taken aback by that, but at the same time impressed. Like me, my father wasn't coming here just to have me survive. He wanted me to thrive, to be the same person I was before I got sick. I didn't come here for a solution so that I could go back to just existing. On the plane ride over and during the darkest days of fighting for my life, I always thought to myself, tomorrow is going to be better. If I can just get to tomorrow, I know I will feel better. I would be up for an hour at a time and dry heaving every five or 10 minutes. It was exhausting, but I was never overwhelmed by it. I wanted relief. Again, I wasn't somebody who let his body go to waste. I got a virus that attacked my heart. My quality of life wasn't what got me in trouble. I was unlucky. I wasn't looking for some way to patch up my body and just get by. That's the attitude I faced in Ontario, and it drove me nuts.

I went in to be examined by Goodwin and my first impression was, well, impressive. Goodwin was impeccably dressed with these big ruby cufflinks. I knew instantly that I was being examined by someone very different from the other doctors I had dealt with. This was a whole new level of health care, something I had never experienced before, particularly during all the months I dealt with my heart problem. I felt comfortable immediately and felt like I was in the presence of an expert. This was like going to the principal's office. You know you have to be on your best behavior and pay close attention to every word that's said. At the same time, it was really hard for me to focus because I felt terrible. I had to gut it out to show him who I was as a person.

The exam wasn't unusual, but the attention to detail was. Goodwin took thorough, copious notes. He took his time because he had no push to do otherwise. There weren't patients stacked up to see him. He saw only the cases he wanted to see and was well paid for it. My visit to Goodwin cost 800 pounds, a huge sum even today. Although England has socialized medicine – the National Health Service, as they call it – Goodwin was one of the doctors who could straddle the line between private and socialized medicine.

At this point, I was seeing him as a private patient. However, for the rest of the time, I was lucky because I still had British citizenship and I was covered under the NHS. With Goodwin, I was really more dependent upon his largesse and his interest in my case than any amount of money I could pay. At this stage of his life, he wasn't about cash, he was about challenge and that was obvious by how he did his work. He meticulously took all of my vital records. He wrote down every detail we could tell him. He had a notebook with my name pre-printed on the label. He listened and listened, prodding occasionally for more details that might give him a clue about me or my treatment.

When he was done, he told me to get dressed and meet him in his office upstairs. He wanted to talk to my parents and me again. The four of us walked out of the examination room and I saw the stairs. Stairs were my nemeses these days. I didn't want to beg out of anything, but Goodwin still sensed I needed some prodding. "My office is upstairs, Simon. Come on, you can do it." Really, it was Goodwin's way of getting a look at how I handled the stairs, the way he examined other patients from time to time.

Goodwin's office was luxurious, an oversized room with rich wood tones and warmth. One wall was covered with oil paintings of the countryside, another with shelves of books neatly arranged, and a third featured all of Goodwin's diplomas and honors. The doctor sat behind an enormous mahogany desk in a deep, rich leather chair. A large, thick-paned window was behind him overlooking the street scene. Goodwin rifled through the large stack of papers that made up my file, jotting notes with a gold pen. Finally, after making me and my parents wait, he gave his analysis.

"Originally, when Dr. Chant wrote me, I thought maybe our doctors could locate the virus and treat it with interferon," he said, referring to yet another drug therapy that was designed to attack viruses and other harmful illnesses. "After deeply examining his files and observing Simon's present condition, I now realize that there is no point in that. The heart has deteriorated to such an extent that even if we cured the virus – a difficult prospect at best – there is not much left of the heart muscle."

At that point, he looked directly at me and said, "Your heart has deteriorated at a faster rate than I anticipated. I'm not confident treatment would help you at this stage." I was wondering why we had come this far. I could have saved the trip and let the rest happen back home.

My father was pointed and asked, "Doctor, if you can't help us, what do we do?"

Fortunately, Goodwin was just getting warmed up.

"Please don't feel your trip has been wasted. I'll see what I can do about getting you on a transplant program. It might be tough because we generally don't treat patients from outside England," he said. My dad reminded him that I'm an English citizen and Goodwin acknowledged that would help. From there, he had to get more information from Vancouver General Hospital, but this was that opening. In soccer parlance, this was like one of those games when you have been "setting up" the man who has been marking you most of the game. You know that at the crucial time near the end of the game, you are going to do something uncharacteristic, something that the defender is unprepared for because you haven't shown it all game. Now, the opportunity you have been waiting for comes. In life, like in games, you have to be ready for that moment. In soccer games you wait for those moments to score; in this game, I had waited to get to get the opportunity to live.

Goodwin told us to come back in a week. While we had been down this path before, at least Goodwin was on the same page with what my doctors at home were saying. He said I needed a heart transplant. On the flipside, I was thinking about a lot of the things that could go wrong. The irritated side of me was taking hold again. I wondered aloud if we were just wasting our time, that they would do more and more tests and then come to the conclusion that they weren't going to help me because I didn't live there.

In truth, Goodwin's approach was just the opposite. After he had gotten done with me, he started looking at another heart patient who was looking for a transplant, a heavy smoker who had already had a triple-bypass operation. Goodwin got annoyed just reading the file. He went back to my file and looked it over again. What Goodwin said he saw was a bigger picture than the numbers or notes that made up my file. He was captured by my attitude. He knew I wasn't going to give up without a fight. I had come all this distance with a purpose. As much as my purpose may have been clouded by circumstance, I was the right candidate for a heart transplant.

As my parents and I took a cab back to my uncle's house, Goodwin picked up the phone and called Dr. English. . English had tilted over more than his share of windmills over the previous decade-plus, fighting through politics to kick-start a heart transplant program that so many other doctors wanted no part of. Goodwin wasn't one of those doctors. Time and again, he had sent English notes of encouragement to keep fighting for the program. Goodwin spoke in support of English. They had a bond that went beyond professional respect and admiration.

English had started the program at Papworth Hospital in Cambridge, roughly 60 miles north of London. It had taken him nearly six years to build a program and finally perform the first surgery in 1979. Think about that: I was about to have surgery in a program that had been up and running for all of seven years. Heck, the first heart transplant wasn't even done until 1967 in South Africa. Even by those standards, I was wading into a field that was just getting past infancy.

But if I was going to make it, I needed to have the right frame of mind. Fortunately, I demonstrated enough of that to Goodwin so that he was willing to fight for me and call in a favor from a colleague. Goodwin knew when he called English that it was English's policy not to operate on people from outside England. He was concerned that his still-budding program couldn't handle the potential bad publicity of using NHS money to care for someone who was skirting the rules on citizenship. Goodwin didn't pull any punches; he told English right away that I was from Canada.

"I'd like to help you, you know that," English said. "But you're well aware of my policy about treating patients from outside England. You're making life difficult."

Again, that's an opening for discussion. English was discouraging, but he wasn't saying no.

"I understand and I can appreciate it," Goodwin countered. "But if you would just see him, I think you'll understand why I'm asking you to make an exception. He's quite an extraordinary young man. He has more than staying alive on his mind. Otherwise, he wouldn't have come halfway around the world for a second chance. We should at least consider his case. Surely, we can give him that much."

English relented and said, "I owe you that much." The arrangements were made. By the next day (not in a week), Goodwin told me I would be going to Papworth to see Dr. English in 10 days. It was another wait for another round of tests and another chance to be turned down. Goodwin made no promises to me about what might happen. At the time, he also didn't tell me how much he worked on my behalf. What I learned from this process was that doctors have to manage expectations, particularly when they don't have final control over the situations.

But when you've spent 18 months waiting and waiting just to find out what's really wrong with you, going through bureaucratic nightmares along the way as you're dying a little more each day, it's hard to keep your attitude focused. I've been through brutal physical training and pushed my body harder than even I thought I could just to play soccer, but this process pushed me further mentally than any of that.

What aggravated the situation at this point was my continuing decline without prednisone. As it became harder for my heart to pump blood through my system, it became harder for me to take in air as well. The associated problem was that any kind of smell or gas or smoke could make me wretch. After taking cabs from Bromley to London the first couple of times, we had to start using the commuter trains which led to London's Underground (or "The Tube" as so many people there call it). For all of its convenience, the Underground is a mixing ground for just about any type of odor. From sweat to smoke to cheap perfume, the air was a concoction seemingly aimed at me. I threw up constantly. Other commuters didn't even notice. It was like standard operating procedure. My mother would make apologies to no one in particular.

Through all of this, my mother kept begging me to take prednisone. I continued to refuse. I had proved to Goodwin how sick I was. Now I had to do the same with yet another doctor and I wasn't going to take the chance.

We arrived early at Papworth Hospital for yet another round of tests. I worked with four attendants during the process, hitting the treadmill yet again and going through the psychological tests. But my immediate perception of Papworth and what its program was about was just the opposite of what I saw in Ontario. Instead of holding my physical fitness (or at least what was left of it) against me, they wanted a patient who was fit in other areas of his body. They wanted to make sure my body was ready to handle the shock of going through a heart transplant.

Likewise, what they wanted from a psychological side was someone who didn't think in terms of limits on their future. Rather, it was about who was going to chase life as hard as possible and return to the life they had before. As I found out later, the greatest success Papworth had early on was Castle, the heavy smoker and drinker who had become a favorite of reporters because he was a character and lived that way even after his transplant.

Though my life was different than Castle's, we both had a sense of determination not to let a heart transplant get in the way of what we wanted to do with our lives. That's what the people at Papworth were looking for. Look, anybody who comes looking for a heart transplant is going to be dealing with some type of anxiety or depression or whatever negativity you want to name. It's just part of the deal. By the time I got to Papworth, I wasn't in a great frame of mind, but I also was still fighting for something at my core. Papworth recognized that in me rather than making me feel like some type of freak because I didn't fit their criteria of what a heart patient was supposed to sound like.

The last person I met that day (along with my parents) was Virginia O'Brien, who was known as Papworth's Transplant Patient Advisor and Rehabilitation Manager. In her own direct way, she was perfect. She knew how to bridge the gap between the technical side of what the doctors were doing and how to make patients understand it. She was perfect for me, direct, no-nonsense and smart. In so many ways, she was like a coach and very much like another woman I met later in life, Sheila Smith, who helped me tremendously. O'Brien didn't wait for me to ask questions, she gave me the answer straight away, including all the downside risks about death and what would happen if I didn't do this or that right after surgery.

She wasn't ordering me around, but she was basically saying my recovery had to be done a certain way or I wasn't going to survive. Again, that's like a great coach saying that you have to play a certain way or you're going to lose. When you hear that, you pay attention.

By my second day at Papworth, I got to see the man, Dr. English. All these years later, English and I have been back in contact. Our first meeting since I left Papworth was 25 years later at my home in Las Vegas, which was a great honor for me. For him, I think it was gratifying as well because it made him know that all the ideas he had way back in the '70s and '80s were right on track. In a funny aside, my wife, Kelly, and I spent three days going through dozens of different specialty food shops looking for the "correct" orange marmalade for his visit because he mentioned it in an email. It was completely inconsequential to him, but I remember driving around Las Vegas asking myself, "How many stores is the right number to find the right marmalade for the man who replaced your heart?"

English is a tall (6-foot-1), lean man with a subdued attitude, much like Goodwin. He was friendly and engaging, but hardly this giant of a character that you would expect for the father of a country's heart transplant program. He fought battles by beating people with a thousand paper cuts rather than slashing them apart with a sword. But that's how you do it in the professional ranks, I suppose. You can't just run over your opponents in the medical field. You have to meticulously fight. That's exactly what English did.

At the same time, English was an intense, driven man who never gave up on his goal. There were a hundred times he could have given up the fight, gone into some other branch of medicine, had a good career and made plenty of money, but he didn't do that. After I finished my tests at Papworth, I was sitting on bed getting dressed. He came in the room, sat on the bed next to me. I had continued my habit of sitting up in bed, thinking I would feel and look a little less sick.

As he started to talk to me, it wasn't like the other conversations I had with other doctors. Looking back, he was clearly there on a different mission. He wasn't talking about deteriorating valves or falling ejection fractions. He was there for have a very different conversation. He was there to deliver a message.

"I've reviewed your case, Simon," English said, putting his hand on the growing stack of papers that made up my file. "And with the tests we've done, we've been able to fully assess your condition."

I've heard this stuff before. I wanted to get to the conclusion. English didn't waste time.

"I'm willing to offer you a transplant, if you'd like it." he said, looking up to see my reaction. I was humbled by the combination of directness and a sense of relief.

I couldn't think of anything to say other than, "Yes, please," as if I was answering one of my teachers in school.

As we continued to talk, a man with a Polaroid camera walked in and took my picture. The people at Papworth kept pictures of the patients as a reminder of whom they were working with. It eventually went into the file as a "before" picture.

English then continued.

"You're sick enough for us to do the transplant if one becomes available immediately. But at the same time, on your present medication, you can continue as you are. So for the time being, you can just go back to London and wait," he said.

I have no idea what got English to change his mind about helping me. Maybe he saw a loophole in the fact that I was a British citizen, allowing him a way to get around the fact that I was Canadian. Maybe he liked my attitude from what he had been told. Maybe he just followed the Hippocratic Oath. Maybe he felt indebted to Goodwin. As I found out later, most patients who had come to Papworth for evaluation went through four days of tests before hearing from English. I got through in only two.

It was June 6, 1986 and now more than three months since I had been originally told I needed a transplant or I would die. At that point, I didn't care what English's justification was and I still don't. I had just arrived at a big moment in my comeback and I was able to score. This was big!

And, frankly, this probably worked out for the best. While I realize that a big part of the problem in Ontario was that I looked to be in better shape because of the prednisone, the fact that I ended up at Papworth with Dr. English was a key to my recovery. I got a great sense that the attitude at Papworth was much more in line with what was going to work for me. In England, it was more, "OK, you're going to have a transplant, no problem, you're going to go back to living your life once you do." It was a directness that bordered on harsh, but the British are more like that. They want to get to the point and get moving. I appreciated that attitude. Here I was being told for 18 months that my heart was a wreck and finally I got to someone who said, "Yep, it's a wreck, let's fix it."

It was a gigantic relief.

That long, uncomfortable plane ride had become so worth it. But I was still a long way from a solution.

9

A LIFE INTERRUPTED

My life is full of odd coincidences intertwined with James Fields. His mom was a P.E. teacher. So was my dad. His family believed in the value of sports, as did mine. His family traveled through North America – particularly the United States – throughout his life, showing the same sense of adventure that my parents taught me and my brothers when we all left England in the 1960s.

And James and I both loved sports.

My first and most impactful encounter with big league soccer occurred in Vancouver, British Columbia, the mainland metropolis across from Vancouver Island where I grew up. The Vancouver Whitecaps were a powerhouse in the North American Soccer League throughout the 70s and 80s, attracting many of England's finest professionals with lucrative contracts. Vancouver was Canada's soccer center. I spent my youth playing soccer at a park less than mile from my home. The road that park sits on? Vancouver Street.

Now, I'm not one of those people who believe in mysticism, but it's hard to ignore certain signs or markings. The soccer pitch on which James Field played his last game in Wales. Less than a mile from his house. The field where he died, was bordered by a road named:

Vancouver Drive.

Then there's my son, Sean. At our first meeting with the Fields family, James' father Robert gazed drop-jawed at Sean.

Finally, after awkward silence, Robert confided his son had had a blaze of red hair, the same hue as Sean's. The tone of Sean's hair is a rarity indeed. From time immemorial, no one in my family, or my wife's family, had ever donned the slightest tint of red hair, either naturally or otherwise.

James had a lot going for him. He was smart, energetic, good-natured, slightly mischievous and very driven to success. He was ahead of his years and by 1986 he had finished his junior year at school.

James was actually born in the U.S., when his father was studying for his PhD at a university in Indiana. Just like my family had done a year before, Paula and Robert Fields came by boat to the United States, to push forward on creating a better life for their family.

They drove all the way from New York harbor to Indiana in an American car, getting up to speed on some new-world oddities like power brakes, air conditioned automobiles and 100 flavors of ice cream. As Paula recalls, every time her husband touched the brakes, their luggage -- piled up high in the back seat -- would slide forward into the back of her head. Now in England, you were lucky if you got three standard choices of ice cream: vanilla, chocolate and strawberry. So it was, during one pit-stop in the Midwest, the Fields' inquired which flavors of ice cream were available. The couple laughed at themselves when the waitress endlessly recited the list from start-to-finish, beginning with boysenberry and blueberry...

James and I were the both the third child born to our parents. Both our parents adore kids. And both taught us a strong work ethic – they taught us by their example.

After having grown their family by three kids by the time Robert had completed his academic work in America, the Fields returned to England. Their family grew by two more kids and eventually they settled in Wales to live a relatively idyllic life. In 1977, they purchased a six-bedroom home, a structure which required plenty of work.

Between lectures and grading papers, Robert was a self-employed contractor. And their large home (approximately 4,000 square feet by

American standards) was in constant need of repair. From wiring to wallpaper and eventually remodeling, there was never an idle moment.

Paula recalls one night they were all working hard to finish wallpapering the ceiling in daughter Kim's bedroom.

"The kids were standing on stools with brushes to hold up the paper so they could brush the paste on the paper," she recalls. "Now I was pregnant at the time, and I was always very sick with my pregnancies. So, I'm going off to be sick, then struggling up from the bed to get back to the kids before the paste on the wallpaper is dry."

Kim recalls, "When we moved to Wales, we used to spend weekends at the do-it-yourself store."

Within this hard-working environment, all of the children have gone on to successful careers.

James was headed down the business path.

"He was by far the most entrepreneurial and he showed it," Robert said.

"I went out to Hong Kong once and James gave me some money and asked, 'Can you please purchase certain polo shirts?' The Fila shirts that were immensely popular in the early '80s. Some top tennis players wore them back then. To have one was very impressive among the kids."

James had it all planned out for his dad.

"Can you go to this family market, and get me some of these, please?" he asked.

"He was very clever," said Robert. "He would wear a shirt for a while, and get the recognition for having them, then he'd sell them off for more than he bought them."

He was just a kid.

"He absolutely loved his tennis clothes and having that fashionable look. We would tease him all the time about how expensive they were, but then he would turn a profit on them and get the last laugh."

James turned the same trick with cassette tapes. He loved The Clash. About three times a year, they'd have this exhibition in town, something like a flea market. A few men would come around and have an indoor market in one of the local hotels to sell bootleg tapes. James would buy the cassettes there, keep some for himself, and make money off the rest.

In the truest sense of the capitalist spirit, James pushed the boundaries. Once, he tried selling lunch coupons that some of the less fortunate children in school received.

"Many of the children at school came from families whose incomes were below a certain level," explained Robert. "Each Monday, these children got five free meal tickets for the week. Other kids who were not entitled to free lunch tickets had to pay for their food. So these tickets had a monetary value. So James would buy a ticket from a kid who had one, then sell it to someone else for slightly more than what he bought it for, but slightly less than the cost of lunch."

Perfectly ingenious. Mischievous? Perhaps.

And, unfortunately, illegal.

Robert happened to be the head of the school's parent association. So to have your kid profiteering on a school nutritional entitlement program didn't play well at the Fields' dinner table.

To his credit, James never pushed back if you told him to stop things. He was going to push it to the limit until it was explained that he had gone too far. It was part of what made him.

James was clever with his relatives, too. His grandfather, on his dad's side, lived in Birmingham and would come to visit with the family whereupon leaving would give each of the children a handful of pocket money. Invariably, James would always get the lion's share. When his siblings complained, his dad remarked:

"Have you asked yourself why? Who spends the most time with their grandpa? Who talks to him, and listens to him? Whether he wants to or not? James does."

Later, his dad explained:

"This was part of his character. OK, he saw an opportunity. That may sound awful, in one respect, but he was just a child. He was doing it out of the goodness of his heart, and was rewarded for it ... He realized which side his bread was buttered. He would curry favor with my father," Robert said. "But James would go to my father's home and tend to the gardens."

Doing all this enabled him to earn enough money to buy his own stereo system. All these years later, the system is still in use in the family room downstairs.

"He had a go-getter mentality," Paula said. "If he had an idea about what he wanted, he had a plan for going after it and he pursued it."

"What he would have done in his later life, I'm not sure," Robert said. "He probably might have followed me and gone into finance or running his own business. His older brother and sister both worked when they were young, but it was different with James. His brother had a paper route, and his sister worked at Woolworth's on the weekend, although she was a good bit brighter than necessary for that for a job by that age. James just had this sense for how to make money -- without having to spend time on a job."

James loved France. He and his older sister traveled there together and handled themselves well on their own. To this day, his sister has trouble talking about her brother. Simply stated, her memories and loss are too painful.

By the time he was 17, James was over 6-feet tall with a long, angular build. Paula would watch him run up the driveway every day after school, charging into the house through the utility room door that led to the kitchen. From there, he would grab onto a bar in the house and practice his pull-ups or hit the floor for push-ups. He'd play in the backyard with the elder of his two smaller brothers, sometimes hitting a tennis ball with him on the lawn in back. During the long lunch periods from school, which were almost two hours back then, he would sometimes come home and take care of the older one, while his mother fed the baby who grew up to bear a striking resemblance to James.

James played tennis constantly with the family, usually his sister.

James' friends admired him. Years after his death, one of them even named his first-born son after James. While he had yet to have a truly serious girlfriend, he had a sweetness many girls were drawn to. After his funeral, a girl named Joanna came to the house and asked if she could have one of

James' scarves to remember him by. Joanna's mother also came to the house and paid James a high compliment in Robert's eyes.

Robert recounts:

"To me, the important thing was what Joanna's mother said. If Joanna went upstairs with James, the mother said she had no worries. She didn't feel that she had to go up and check if they were behaving properly. I thought that was very nice. It was a sweet thing of her to say to us. She trusted James. To me that tries to reinforce the idea that he was a softer, more kindly person. He used to take on the role of bodyguard of his youngest sibling as well if he thought he was being got at by the other younger brother."

"He was serene, a completely pleasant young man," Paula said. "There wasn't a cruel bit to him. Mischievous at times, but never anything harmful … really, he had an idyllic childhood in so many ways, and he was a perfect young man."

Sadly, no one is perfect. James had a congenital problem with the circulation of blood in his brain. It was something the family never knew until it was too late. On Sunday, July 6, 1986, everything in James' life came to a crashing halt.

The night before, the neighbors to the side of the house where James' bedroom was located had a party. The next day, the same neighbors had a luncheon and invited the Fields family. "It was a lovely day," Paula said. James had complained of a headache, which wasn't surprising because of the party the night before. He took a couple aspirin as Paula and Robert sat down to watch the Wimbledon men's final. It was a classic match between Ivan Lendl, the No. 2 player in the world at the time, and Boris Becker, the 18-year-old German sensation who was No. 1 and the defending champion. At 17, Becker had become the youngest man to ever win the title, and his sudden rise had attracted much attention and enthusiasm. He played with zest, and an athletic style that was both exciting and endearing, particularly when compared to the controlled style of Lendl, who played with the passion of a tax collector. From a spectator perspective, it was easy to draw a line between good and bad when watching them play.

The three-set match was fantastic, as Paula recounts. The third and final set went to a tiebreaker. The day wore on into evening, and Becker closed in on his second straight title.

The Fields children weren't as enraptured, and the two youngest boys went to play soccer in the backyard.

Then James decided to head four blocks down the road to the neighborhood park to play soccer with some friends.

Sometime later, one of James' friends came running up to the door.

"Something has happened to James and he won't get up!" the boy said, breathlessly.

Paula initially thought it might be a broken leg or something like that as she headed out the door. Robert stayed back with the younger children and Paula found out just how grave the situation was. Her son lay on the soccer pitch, not moving and not responding to CPR. An ambulance was called and the couple soon found out it was an aneurysm. A blood vessel in James' brain had burst, filling the cranium with blood as it hemorrhaged.

At the hospital, the couple faced the worst horror of any parent, having to deal with the death of a child.

"This is one of the hardest things for me to remember," Robert recalled. "I sat there looking at the inert body, willing it to come alive again. You know it isn't going to happen, but it doesn't stop you from hoping."

Twenty-five years later, this memory causes Robert to break down in tears, bowing his head to hide his face and regain his composure.

"Really, when I look back on it, he was the one who lost so much, not me," Robert said, trying to deflect the sorrow and pity. "We have all gone on and had wonderful lives. He's the one who didn't get that."

The immediate aftermath of James' death was a whirlwind for the family. However, one of the first considerations was whether to donate his organs. To the couple, the choice went without saying.

"I don't understand how people have a problem with donation," Paula said. "If you cared for a child, why would you waste all that caring if somebody else could benefit? I can't say I consciously thought about that at the time that James died. But there was just this overwhelming feeling of: 'I can't waste this, I can't waste this.' Somebody else has to benefit from this loss."

"But after we had made the decision, the donation didn't help relieve the grief. It was logical, it was the only thing to do."

As a mother, looking at him lying in the bed, I remember his hands were on top of the blanket, and his nails were beautiful. He had lovely hands. I remember thinking all the caring I had done for my boy for 17 years. I made sure he'd brushed, and he'd done his hair, and I thought all this cannot just go to waste.

That was my only thought: How much love and care I had had for my son. It was just instinctive to say yes to organ donation. We had actually discussed this in the family because Kim had a donor card, which she got from school, and I remember James saying, 'When I'm 18, I'm going to get one of those.'

The problem was, James didn't have a donor card and, back then, it was impossible to be a donor without going through a massive legal rigmarole. So with raw emotions, Robert and Paula went through the process.

"You had to say yes to each item," Robert said. "I was thinking: 'Cut the crap, we already said yes!' "

"They started asking about the corneas, and this and that and this and that, and I remember at one point just shouting at the guy, saying, 'It's not a shopping list, take what you want!' Then they ask you if you want to know where everything goes, and we said no."

Paula said, "I remember quite clearly driving home from the hospital thinking I'm going home to a terrible house of grief. "Weeks later, we got a letter saying where the organs had been used.

"Two families were going to get kidneys, and all I was thinking was how overjoyed they and their loved ones are going to be. I remembered reading a book called *The Prophet* by Khalil Gibran, and he has a wonderful piece about joy and sorrow. One person's sorrow is another person's joy, and that's how I think of it. I found it really useful reading that after James died. To suffer means that you have loved. If you didn't love, you didn't suffer. It's a lovely book. So I can remember that overriding the grief, and then the tremendous family support that came with this. It was just amazing. Even though it was such a difficult, horrible time."

Donating never changed the grief.

"I wish I could endorse the statement that donation eases grief, but it doesn't. Grief is grief. The only positive thing that came out of this is what happened for Simon, and I'm glad for that."

A short distance away in London, I was about to get the heart I so desperately needed. I ended up getting what would be the perfect heart. Again, this was of little solace to the Fields family, whose pain has never vanished.

The immediate years were the most difficult. Their oldest son dealt with the sorrow for a long time. Their daughter dealt with it, but she refuses to talk about James to strangers.

One of the younger sons – the one who resembled James the most – made a remark years later. He came down from his room one day with a sense of relief. His mother asked him what was on his mind and he said, "I've finally lived longer than James." For years, he silently thought that he might suffer the same fate as his brother since they were so much alike.

Paula dealt with her own issues. For months afterward, she would wake up from terrible nightmares.

"I'd go to the hospital and James would be in bed. I would say to the nurse, 'I'll take him home now.' She'd say to me, 'You can't Mrs. Fields, don't you remember? You gave away his heart.' I would wake up the family at night screaming, and today my children are still very concerned about me talking about this

"This went on for ages. So to cope, I would think of James when he was happy, and imagine him running up the drive, as he used to when he came back from school, or how he used to pull himself up on the doorframe in the kitchen. Every time I got that horrible picture of him from the nightmare, I'd over-stamp it with a good picture.

"Gradually the bad pictures faded, and when I thought about James, it was just the good pictures that came.

"I don't know how other people cope with the loss of a child. We were of the era when there was no counseling, nothing at all. My kids got no counseling. If that happened now – any death of a sibling – the children would immediately get counseling. They would have had help with it. My kids had no help with it. My husband and I had no help with it.

Years later, when having the opportunity to meet with Simon and his family, having learned he was the recipient of James' heart, Robert for one, was overjoyed to learn of the good the donation had produced. The chance to meet Simon and his family gave Robert some comfort.

But each summer, as the early days of July tick by, Paula's unable to bring herself to watch the Wimbledon men's final.

"It has been 25 years, but I just can't do it."

10

The World Cup and the One-Legged Man

It is a strange thing to wait for someone to die so that you might live. Really stop and think about that for a second. What an awful prospect. In its very essence, that's where I was in my life by the middle of May 1986. That's a weird place to be at age 20. After 18 months of first trying to figure out what was wrong and then trying to convince someone to approve me for a transplant, here I was finally on the list for a heart. Of course, getting on the list is a long way from a guarantee.

Plenty of people who need transplants die waiting, whether you're waiting for a heart or kidneys or whatever it is. The timing doesn't work. The right person with the right-sized organ with the right blood type doesn't always die in time. This is not like the movies where the miracle always happens. The helicopter with the guy carrying some small ice chest doesn't always land on time, let along even take off. Yeah, there's plenty of tension and worry and drama – more than enough to fill the Hallmark Channel with material for years to come. But, in some sense, the stars have to align, at least for the person in need. For the donor, the circumstance is almost always tragic and that goes without saying if you're talking about a heart transplant.

In the immediate aftermath of meeting Dr. English in May 1986 and having him offer to put me on the transplant list, my dad and I were as close to euphoria as you could imagine. As I said before, we were like the coach and player looking at that breakthrough moment in the game when the comeback was on. My dad exulted by saying, "At last!" and I kept talking about what great news this was. My mother, as usual, was worried, not sure how she would get through it. I just kept reassuring her by repeating how great the moment was.

We walked the grounds of the hospital back to meet with some other administrators for a briefing on what was supposed to happen if and when I got called. I wasn't thinking about "if" at that point. There was a bulletin board of news clippings the nurses had put up about successful transplants that had happened. I figured there would be a story about me up there soon. I toured the intensive care unit and then met with Virginia O'Brien again.

This time, she gave me the serious pre-game talk. She pulled me aside to talk without my parents around and make sure I was comprehending the whole process.

"I know this hurts and is quite difficult, but do you really understand what is going to happen to you in the next few months?" she said. "The ones who don't understand and say they do are asking for trouble because they are the same ones who get into difficulty later and say, 'nobody told me this' or 'I don't remember anybody ever mentioning that.' This is a big investment, Simon."

I told her I knew that and I was ready. She wasn't done.

"Do you really fully grasp everything I'm telling you and everything we're showing you?" she said, looking straight into my eyes to read me. She wanted to know that I was committed to every step, including taking the anti-rejection medicine I would need for the rest of my life. She had run into plenty of patients who went back to their old habits after getting a transplant, such as drinking and/or smoking heavily and eating poorly. I get where she was coming from, but I don't think she really understood who I was yet. That wasn't what got me to this point. Still, she wasn't done giving me an earful. This was a serious pep talk.

Finally, I said to her: "Really, I do get it. Let's just do it – let's get on with it. I have a life to get on with."

That resonated with her.

"Good," she said. "The people who come here have to want to get better. It's not enough for people who have a transplant operation to say, 'I don't want to die.' They have to actually say, 'By God, I want to live, I've got so much to live for.' I can see you are one of these people."

The other thing the hospital does – or at least what it did back then before cell phones were big – is give you a pager to let you know when it's time to go to the hospital. We didn't get one for the first couple of days. Instead, they said they would call us at my aunt and uncle's house in Bromley. Suffice to say, the phone didn't ring twice at the house until the pager arrived a few days later.

I didn't have the pager. My parents carried it. The pager becomes the center of your life. You check to make sure you have the pager. You check to make sure the pager is working right. You check to make sure the pager is on. You look at the batteries. You look at the pager every time you wake up to check if it went off and somehow you didn't hear it.

It's like getting a pager at a restaurant, but then multiply that feeling times a million. At a restaurant, you might wait for 30 or 45 minutes and you're checking the pager a few times. Think about that over a span of months with your life on the line – or worse, your child's life on the line. My mom used to call every couple of days just to check and O'Brien told her: "If there was news, you would know about it. We don't sit on it for three days."

For me, the reaction was to become indifferent. I'm not saying I was indifferent to life. I was indifferent to the little details that don't matter over the course of a day or a week or whatever you're talking about. "Whatever" became my favorite word. Something is broken. Whatever. The cab is late. Whatever. We're not going to eat until later. Whatever.

I wanted to live and I wanted very badly to return to my life, but this was the time when it wasn't worth sweating the small things. I imagined kicking a soccer ball again. I imagined competing. At the end of May that year, the month-long World Cup started in Mexico. This was supposed to be a year of great achievement for Canada, a time to truly rejoice. For the first time ever, our country was playing in the World Cup. To this day, it's the only time we have played in the tournament. I kept thinking that this World Cup was supposed to be my chance, that I could have been out there with the team if not for getting sick. All these years later, I know it was my golden opportunity and my health didn't allow it.

I'm not bitter about that in the least. That's the way it goes. Soccer was too great for me to look back in anger. In fact, it was probably my conditioning from soccer that allowed me to live to see the end of that World Cup. It was playing soccer and competing at a high level that created the attitude I presented and made doctors such as Goodwin and English take notice of me. They weren't saving me because I was some great player, mind you. They were saving me because I had a desire to make something of my life and return to live it to the fullest. Soccer also helped me survive once I did get the transplant. Back then, the rate of success for someone surviving even a year post-surgery was 70 percent. In other words, it wasn't like I was getting a guarantee even once I had the surgery. Frankly, you have better odds surviving Russian Roulette than surviving 2 years after a heart transplant. It didn't matter to me. I was focused on making this work.

In the immediate time after meeting with Dr. English at Papworth, my parents and I went back to my uncle Malcolm and aunt Laurette's home in Bromley. For the most part, the situation was pleasant. I was with family and my parents had relatives who could help out. We mostly stuck to the house because it was hard for me to go out and my parents were tied to the beeper.

The problem with the arrangement is that as the days grew into weeks and then tipped past a month. By early June, the wear and tear on the relationship between my parents and my aunt and uncle started to show. Uncle Malcolm liked a drink. So did Laurette. They weren't irresponsible about it or anything. They just like to come home, relax and each of them throw down a bottle of sherry on most nights. Malcolm liked some ale, too. Not a problem. He liked to smoke a fair share and watch some TV.

Well, for the month we were there, my mom slowly put a kibosh on all of that behavior. At least the TV and the smoking. She couldn't say much about the drinking. Again, to me, whatever. The smoking wasn't really good for me and I was getting to a stage that even the slightest of any smell was making me heave. It was getting tougher and tougher for me to deal with. But we were living at their house. They were being incredibly gracious. But my mom was defending her child and I get that. I could imagine what my wife Kelly would do now if one of our kids were sick. She would do what she had to do, even if it stepped on some toes along the way.

Malcolm started grousing that I was being "overclucked" by my mom the mother hen. When they played cards, my mother would try to get everybody to be quiet so I could sleep. Malcolm responded by saying: "He would probably sleep better if you weren't checking up on him every two minutes. Why don't you just leave the kid alone? He'll call you if he needs anything." When Laurette tried to help me and my mother interceded, Malcolm got testy again. My father played the role of Switzerland between his wife and his brother, but everybody's nerves were getting stretched thin by the proximity and the anxiety.

I also helped keep things quiet because it was hard to get too angry when you have somebody dying in the next room. I couldn't eat much from day to day, throwing up almost as soon as I ate something. The nausea was constant and the breathing was difficult. The World Cup games would be about the only distraction that could take my mind off the discomfort for any stretch of time.

The final of the World Cup was my breaking point. On June 29, everyone got ready to watch Argentina play West Germany for the title (Argentina ended up winning, 3-2). England had lost in the quarterfinals to Argentina, in the match featuring the infamous "Hand of God" goal by maestro Diego Maradona. All of England was sure that this was the year that it would repeat its historic 1966 title. To have it snatched away by the hated Argentinians was almost too much to bear. The English were an excellent squad that year and had a real chance to lift the famed Cup. Imagine being in England and watching Argentina play West Germany in the World Cup Final. The Brits had a long-standing hatred for the Argentines on the soccer field. Then there were the Germans, who the English still harbored ill feelings for from World War II. Most of England probably wanted the game to end with no winner.

For me, I didn't care one tiny bit. I was ready to break. I was upstairs resting in my room. This was the order of the day now since things were getting tougher and tougher for me.

Outside, Malcolm and Laurette barbecued dinner. I hadn't eaten much in the past three or four days. I just couldn't keep anything down. Now, the fumes from the barbecue wafted to the upstairs window and were too much for me to bear. I yelled for my father and said; "I don't think I can take it anymore. The smell – the fumes are making sick. I can't take it." After nearly two months of living with my aunt and uncle, I had to go. It wasn't their fault. You can't expect people to live like they're in a hospital for two months. It wasn't right for me to be there anymore. Frankly, I needed to be in a place where there was better care, where there was quiet, where people weren't, you know, trying to live a normal life.

My father called the general practitioner, Dr. Ross Ellice, to see where they could move me. Ellice got me into King's College Medical Hospital in south London, where there was a fine cardiologist to look after me as I continued to get ill. My first clue that I was going downhill fast was I was taken there by ambulance. The odd part is that when we arrived, there was nobody in the waiting room or in the X-ray department. The place was empty, not even patients. Think about that long and hard for moment, significant parts of a hospital in a major world city were barren of people. It was 6:30 p.m., thirty minutes after the start of the World Cup final. That's how much of a grip soccer has on the world.

This is one of the rare times I ever saw my dad lose his temper. We finally found one doctor in the emergency ward, an East Indian guy who didn't seem interested in the match. My dad told him to admit me right away, but he tried to examine me. That's when my dad yelled, "We know what's wrong with him – he's waiting for a heart transplant!" That pretty much cut to the chase. The problem was they couldn't find the doctor I was supposed to meet. Instead, five interns made their way in and out of the room they put me in, all of them listening to my heart. It was as if they were in some type of medical relay race with me as the baton. Finally, the East Indian doctor returned instead of the specialist I was supposed to see and my father reached his boiling point again.

"I don't want anybody else coming in here checking my son's heart. We know what's wrong with him, stop your B.S. and get him admitted right now. If you don't, I'll have your head," he said. I didn't get a private room, but they put me at the end of the 24-bed ward near the bathroom. It was me and like 19 other guys. I was the only white guy in there. I have no idea why and it didn't matter, it was just odd. It was this big, poorly lit room with all of us in there. The place looked more like a train station than a hospital. In the background, the World Cup game was blaring. Opposite my bed was an 80-year-old man who was an amputee. His prosthetic leg was thrown under his bed. The whole place had that nasty stench of urine and sweat that was more acute because it was stifling hot. In the middle of all this, London was dealing with a heat wave that made everybody that much more uncomfortable. The guy in the next bed died while I was there. It felt like I was in some kind of war movie or something.

That's the last thing I remember.

The World Cup and the one-legged man.

The next eight days, leading up to my life-saving surgery, were a pins-and-needles experience for my parents as they kept watch over me. I wasn't in a coma or anything, but I was delirious and have little recollection of anything that happened up until surgery, including the near-fatal shower I had the next day.

My parents left the hospital at 11 p.m. to return to Bromley, which is about 40 minutes away. Visitor hours were over and they needed some sleep. They came back the first thing the next morning, barely getting any rest. They were hoping that the specialist would finally come see me that night, but no go, he wasn't around. By the next morning, I was lying there feeling sticky and hot. I hadn't showered in I don't know how long because the last thing you're supposed to do when your heart is in the kind of distress mine was in is take a shower.

Particularly a cold shower. Evidently, in my state of delirium, I got the idea that I wanted a shower and told the nurse. She didn't know any better because I didn't exactly have a chart or any records around to say why I was even there. She helped me to the shower, turned on the water and left me there. The shower was tiny. I had lost 30 pounds since I had gone off prednisone and I wasn't that big to begin with. I'm 5-foot-8 and when I got to England in the middle of May, I was 175 pounds. By the time I had surgery on July 7, I weighed 130.

So I was somewhere close to 130 and still barely fit into the shower. I was in there for maybe three minutes and it felt great. To have some cold water on my skin felt just awesome. But when I made my way back to my bed, I almost collapsed from being light-headed. The cold water had raised my heart rate so much compared to what my heart could handle that I was in serious trouble now.

I grabbed the rails of the bed to keep myself from falling. Eventually, I got myself back on the bed and then the tightness hit my chest. I could breathe, but I couldn't exhale. At that point, my dad had just arrived and was watching me (he and my mother started taking turns so the other could get some rest) and was back in action, calling for help.

"This patient needs oxygen, now," my father called out. The attending nurse looked at my chart and told my dad, politely, that she couldn't do it because she didn't have a doctor's signature.

My dad, growing less polite by the second, yelled: "Don't be so God damn stupid. He's going to die unless you give him oxygen."

The nurse said no again and now my dad was in seek-and-destroy mode. He demanded to see the doctor in charge. The nurse said he was "somewhere" in the hospital. While all this is going on, I'm struggling, increasing the anxiety for my dad. He ordered the nurse to page the doctor and then went looking himself. The nurse left and found the doctor, and by the time he arrived, ordered oxygen for me and took my pulse, I was at an extremely low rate and clearly in major distress.

I spent two more days in the general ward before finally getting moved to the acute cardiac care area. I have no recollection of this, but it was a lot better by my parents account. My mom and dad said I kept asking for another shower because of the unrelenting heat. Every time I asked, I was told "tomorrow," everybody knowing another shower with cold water would have probably killed me.

To say that things were getting desperate would be an understatement. One day, my parents went out for tea for a few minutes, only to return to find me sprawled on the floor, blood running down from a cut on my leg. I had fallen while getting out of bed to try for another shower. My parents toyed with the idea of putting me in a private hospital for more observation, but they were shot down, a doctor telling them that if they did that, Papworth would take me off the donor list. This was the politics of Britain's health care system. The logic went that if I had enough money to go to a private hospital, why should the government pay for my heart transplant?

My parents made do. They would move me around constantly to help the pain subside. The work was so constant that the shifts would go for 15 minutes at a time. I was dehydrated, the skin around my eyes getting tight and almost crispy. Unable to use water to bathe me, my mom put lotion on my skin to keep it moist. After she wiped my legs and feet, I would collapse with exhaustion. My dad would roam the hospital to steal every bit of ice he could find, crushing it into a slushy mixture and putting it in my mouth to get me as much water as I would possibly handle, which wasn't much. In their rare free moments, my mom and dad would do crosswords. According to them, every once in a while I would wake up just long enough to suggest an answer and then drift back to sleep. Imagine if you can, watching your until-recently vibrant, athletic son reduced to a skeleton of himself as he dies a little bit more right before your eyes. The pain and horror was excruciating for them.

As the first weekend of July approached, there were evidently some people around the hospital who didn't think I'd make it past Sunday. They obviously didn't say anything to my parents at the time, but they mentioned it later. Likewise, my mother was starting to fear the worst. Back at Malcolm and Laurette's house in Bromley, she broke down in tears during dinner one night and said: "We won't leave him there to die, will we? We'll bring him home here to die. We'll look after him."

Laurette was taken aback by the thought of her two young boys being exposed to someone dying in the house like that. Later that night, my mother continued to lose hope. She couldn't sleep and woke up my dad. "He's not going to make it. I know he's not going to make it," she cried.

I had become so sensitive to any smell because my body was so desperate for oxygen that my mom couldn't even wash her hands with scented soap.

When Laurette and Malcolm came to visit, shocked to see how emaciated I had become, I started saying, "'moke, 'moke" and pointed desperately to the oxygen mask. I could smell the cigarette smoke on their clothes. They had to leave the room in seconds.

On the Friday of that weekend, the hospital nutritionist came by with a box of Nestle nutrition drinks. There might have been a dozen in the box. Whatever it was, my mom said they kept feeding those to me as fast as I could drink them. They'd pour them over ice and give them every time I was awake for more than a few seconds.

"I think it's the only thing that kept him alive," mom said. "The people in the hospital knew how desperate the situation was."

Through the weekend, I clung to life as my parents went through their usual motions of caring for me, talking to the nurses, resting and then repeating. My mother looked at my pale skin and rubbed the limp flesh on my arms and legs that used to be muscle.

They were so in-tune with this process that they failed to notice a flurry of action around me on Monday morning. Doctors and nurses were coming in and out of the room, checking my vital signs. Finally, a doctor stopped and spoke to my parents. He looked stern, which threw my parents off for a second.

"I have some news," he said. "We've had a call from Papworth. We've been in touch all day. We've been instructed to prepare him for Papworth. They think they have a donor. The ambulance is on its way. You had better pack his things."

It was July 7. The day before, approximately 150 miles away, James Fields had passed away suddenly while playing soccer. It was an awful tragedy. It ripped a hole in a family.

It was also the break I desperately needed to survive. It's a harsh equation in which I was the beneficiary. No sane, right-thinking person would ever wish that any family would suffer like this for his own benefit. But after 18 months of suffering, nearly 10,000 miles of flying around Canada and then across the Atlantic Ocean and me coming as close to death as anyone could possibly imagine, this was a moment for my parents to rejoice.

They danced like children on the last day of school. My mother screamed, "At last!" My father yelled, "Finally." As for me, I had no energy to enjoy the moment. I woke up for a second and evidently asked, "Did the beeper go off?" My father said they called instead and talked to the doctors.

All I could do was fall asleep.

11

A MOMENT OF TRUTH

I had what you what you could call two "awakenings" after my heart surgery. The first was when I actually woke up in Papworth Hospital, alive and actually feeling that way for the first time. I had blood flowing through my body with relative ease for the first time in I didn't know how long. While I'm sure I was a little groggy those first few days, it wasn't anything like the previous couple of months.

From the time I was moved from King's College Hospital to when I woke up at Papworth, which was about 36 hours, I don't remember much. I have a faint recollection of them prepping me for surgery at Papworth, because they shaved my whole body with the exception of my head.

Somehow, I remember this part of my ordeal because it happened to conjure another odd and humorous memory. There was, at the time, a long-standing tradition in soccer that whoever was the rookie of the team would get "hazed." Most teams frown on hazing because it has gotten out of control. When it's innocent, it's fine. On many teams that I was on, hazing included the shaving of the areas south of the belt line. Although it happened on many teams that I had been on, I had always been able to dodge the bullet.

In fact, just a summer ago I was on a Provincial Men's team in Canada and I dodged the bullet by only a month. My friend Brian Penk secured the honors. I still remember being in Calgary on that team watching the poor kid get shaved by the veterans. As quietly as I could, I stood in the back trying my best to not get noticed. Well, finally my streak ended at Papworth!

Upon getting prepped for surgery, I turned to my mom and announced in my delirium: "Hey Mom, I am the rookie!"

Rest assured, I was out of it. In fact, for a moment during that time, I *was* literally dead as they took my degenerated, diseased heart out of my body and replaced it with the one I got from James Fields. In a larger sense, I had been out of it for nearly 10 days from my last real memory of watching the World Cup in the midst of getting transferred to the hospital.

Everything else was a blur. I remember two things about the moment I woke up on July 8: I was thirsty as hell and my brother Marc was there. I'd never been so happy to see him. In the rush of getting me to surgery, my parents had called my brothers to fly to England. It was either going to be some great bit of news or for a final chance to say goodbye.

Before I get into the initial part of recovery, I want to mention the key moment or what I call my actual awakening from this whole experience. It's one of those life moments – what I call a Moment of Truth – where everything seems to click, even if this moment was hardly what you would call a success.

About three weeks after surgery, in late July 1986, I had been discharged from Papworth and we had rented a little house in Cambridge where I was working on recuperation. I was still doing what I call the "old man rehab" and was walking around, feeling good, with no significant problems of any kind. I was beginning to think about getting in shape to play soccer again. I was regaining confidence in my body. Again, before I went to England in May, I was looking ahead to the soccer season that September.

Now, it's late July and I'm figuring I better start busting my ass in training or else I might not be ready for September. Of course, this all relates to my theory of the "Power of Stupid," but what the hell. I was 21 and had no clue what I was really doing.

The temperature in England had come back down from that late-June/early-July heat wave. I was still doing some pretty typical heart rehabilitation stuff, but nothing that would remotely qualify as strenuous. It was a somewhat chilly and foggy morning when I snuck out. My mom was in the rental house and was still a little overprotective of me. Her idea was to wrap me up in cotton wool, then a blanket, more cotton wool and put me on the chair so I wouldn't break. I guess I couldn't blame her, but I knew differently. I was ready to go. Dressed in some workout clothes, which was pretty normal, I snuck out of the house. I just walked casually until I reached a park and was out of her sight. Like most communities in the UK, there was no shortage of soccer fields in this neighborhood. As I reached this park, there were acres and acres of soccer fields. Maybe 15 or 20 fields.

Here was my chance to push it. I was going to run. I figured I would keep it to a light jog at first. You know, keep it sensible and not get too out of control. I figured I'd go a couple of miles and stretch my legs just enough and give the new ticker a try. I was feeling strong again and looking ahead to real training. The fact that I had just had my heart taken out of my chest and replaced three weeks earlier didn't really register at that moment. Oh, to be 21 and have an infinite amount of stupidity!

And off I went. Man, did I feel alive. I was free. I was invigorated. I could see my warm breath against the chilly, foggy air. The hospitals, the doctors, the nurses and even the media back home, they were all gone. The frustrations that had built up over two plus years. The poking and the prodding. The questions of my ability to run again. To play again. For an instant they were all gone. It was just me, doing what my body wanted to do so much. It was fantastic.

The first 10 yards were so freeing. Simply awesome. At about 30 yards, my legs started burning. My chest got tight, my side seized up. My body said, "Yo, dude, are you freaking stupid?" I pushed through it, figuring the pain would go away and that it was just a matter of breaking through. At 60 yards, the fire inside my body started. My legs, my chest, my arms, my shoulders … everything was on fire. At 80 yards, the voice that athletes have been trained to ignore started to argue with my body. An inferno was raging inside my body now. My new heart felt like it was going to burst through my chest.

And then it was over. Born free this was not. At 100 yards, I was toast, done. I put my hands on my knees, hunched over in agony. The universal sign of an athlete exhausted. I was pissed. My body had failed me again. I was discouraged, mad, sad, hopeless.

But only for a moment.

As I stood there, hunched over, I was a shadow of the world-class athlete I had been until recently. Alone in some dreary English park 5,000 miles from my home. Away from friends and family. Away from the media scrutiny.

Away from the doctors and nurses. Away from other players, teammates and coaches. I made a decision. The determination welled up inside of me.

All the lessons from my father, all the competitiveness I had developed over the years with my brothers, all the understanding of my body and what I could do when I was healthy completely aligned.

This was *that* moment for me. A Moment of Truth.

This was that time when my desire to push forward at every moment became my greatest ally. I knew right then that I was at an absolute zero in terms of physical condition. In order to come back, I was going to have to come *all the way back* from literally zero to become myself again. I would have to face judgment and scorn, nervousness and curious stares, stereotypes and prejudices. It would take sacrifice, dedication, desire, blood and sweat, but I was going to make it back.

This was the ultimate challenge of my life, and I was ready.

This became the single most important moment in my early life.

Many who face death and survive talk about such moments. This was the ultimate character test for me.

I had a choice to make.

It would have been easy to accept that I was now broken, that I was somehow different and that people would understand if I was never the same again.

As I had these thoughts about accepting that fate, I just got more and more pissed off.

I decided then and there, once and for all, that neither my illness nor my subsequent transplant were going to define me. Not a chance. I told myself, "I'm going to beat this," whatever that meant. I would beat it. I would beat it with passion, pride and commitment.

As I worked through my recovery – I stayed in England until September – I pushed myself a lot harder than the therapists were pushing me. We would do one set of exercises and I would be pushing for the next one. The therapist kept trying to hold me back for the first week, but I knew what my body could handle. It got so bad that my Dad had to step in. I had gone through three therapists in the first week or so and so my Dad had a meeting with the chief of the department. He tried to explain that I was…ummm… "different." She finally got it when he explained it this way: "Simon will push you. He will push his body. He knows his limits. He will push and push and push. He will push you to the wall … and then he will push you through it." Once she understood who I was, I was put in charge of my own therapy.

The good thing in all of this was that I stayed in England for over two months, most of that time spent in what was essentially a halfway house, a combination of part-hospital and part-residential facility for people who were recovering from surgery. I wanted to go home strong, completely rehabilitated. I wanted the people in Victoria to see that there was nothing wrong with me and I was back to normal. But I also got tired of the halfway house and all the protocol. Again, I didn't feel like I needed to deal with all the restrictions. If they had just assessed me physically, they would have seen how much healthier I was than most people there. Here I was, 21 years old and a recovering athlete. I wasn't some 50-year-old, hard-line drinker who had beaten the crap out of his body.

There is feeling among people who have been through transplants and come that close to death that we will often say we "see" or understand things with a clarity that other people don't. I supposed it's this ultimate form of wisdom or whatever else you get from going through this type of situation. I don't really know how to explain it to people when I talk about it, but when I'm around other people who have had transplants, they intuitively understand. It's as if you take that "whatever" attitude you have been through as you're dealing with illness and possible death – that approach I had used to ignore the mundane parts of a day when I first got to England and was staying with my aunt and uncle – and added the euphoria of having survived. You're still indifferent to the small details, but you're also aware of how great the big picture can look. It's like you strip away all the other issues and see things very clearly.

At that moment, I saw what I needed to do.

I needed to get my body back in shape. I needed to play again. I needed to have control over my body to the fullest extent possible. There have been countless other times that I have gone through that in my life. I went through it again when I retired as a professional soccer player. I went through that when I realized that Kelly was the right woman for me, the first woman who completely captured my soul.

I went through the same thing when I finished my degree in college and started my business. I went through the same thing when I decided to write this book. I knew what I needed to get done, and I did it.

But let me get back to the time immediately after surgery.

So I wake up to seeing my brother Marc there. He had flown over as soon as possible from Vancouver. He was working at a hotel at the time and they completely understood the situation. For Marc, this was really important. He's very family-oriented and a little more open about his feelings. He has a great sense of unity for our family, and every family needs that.

Adam got there three days after my surgery because he was in California in a tournament at the time and getting flights out was a little harder. When I saw him, it was encouraging and actually pretty amusing. Adam was sure that when he arrived, he was going to see me bedridden, emaciated and strung with tubes like a giant marionette. He was expecting a horror show. Instead, when he first walked in, we literally bumped into each other in the hallway. He was totally taken aback to see me up and walking around. He looked at me and said, "What are you doing?" My overwhelmed, sincere and full-of-joy response was to say, "Taking a pee." And off I went to the bathroom.

To have those guys there was so important. That was all part of the recovery, that feeling of euphoria. And let me say that it was complete euphoria. I cared again. Not that I had given up when I was at King's College, but this was a new level of excitement. I wanted to actually move around, whereas I just couldn't do that when I was in King's College. All I cared about then was surviving. Now, I was thinking about thriving.

I was hungry again. I started asking, "What's for dinner?" just because I was excited about eating.

At the same time, I didn't ask anybody what had happened during the days I was delirious. I just took their word for it because it was too much to even try to figure out.

Once I had the heart transplant, being at Papworth was actually a beautiful experience. Not only are the grounds of the hospital completely lush, surrounded by weeping willows and duck ponds, but the surrounding

116

area was serene. It's the kind of place where you drive five miles and it's nothing but gorgeous countryside, then you turn a corner and there's a pub. Then you drive for another five miles, turn, and then there's another pub.

I would sit around the grounds for hours just feeding the ducks. They would come right up to the room. With my family there, it was almost like a holiday, except for that little recuperation thing. And really, after all the anxiety, even that was nothing. My parents were relieved, my brothers were relieved, all of the emotion was drained out of the situation and we could all take a deep breath.

For the first time in I don't know how long I felt fully alive again. There was color in my hands and feet. I had some energy again. I could breathe with ease and get air fully into my lungs. I'm not saying I was ready to do a handspring. But it was just this feeling that I was on the right track. I was finally getting healthy instead of getting worse.

I was thinking to myself that the people in Victoria who had been told about the surgery, must have thought I was going through hell. I laughed about that, thinking, "they have no idea how good I feel right now compared to where I was just a little while ago." I was sitting in the sun, looking at these wonderful gardens and thinking how this was so awesome. I had gone from this desperate, awful situation to having a second chance. I went from knocking on heaven's door to feeling like I had my own slice of heaven.

The people at the hospital said the reason I felt so good was because of the medication. I didn't really buy that at the time because I was still feeling so great. They weren't giving me anything that would make me that high for that long. But it was an unbelievable feeling. I would wake up expecting to be sick and in pain, but it never happened. Ever. As I met more and more transplant recipients it was a common theme in recovery. A 10-day period of absolute euphoria. I was enjoying it.

Everything about this was great, except for the other patients. They just didn't seem to get it. In my opinion, their attitudes were totally wrong. They didn't understand how well they were being treated. There was this one guy who was typical of what I saw from so many people. He was this tall guy, probably 6-foot-2 and so white that he looked like a milk bottle. He had had his transplant about a month before I did, and he had been at Papworth for about a month or so when I first showed up. He was also still there when I left. He would walk around and his parents would follow him, picking up after him the whole way. Or they'd give him his robe. He loved the attention, I could just see it. Then again, he had probably been sick all his life, so he had a different state of mind than I did. He kept talking about how he had two goals when he got better. One was going to Ascot for the horse racing. The other was to buy a dog. I looked at him and said: "Man, you don't want to overdo it. Be careful there." He actually thought I was serious.

At the other end of the spectrum was Tommy Verna. He was in the room next to mine. He was probably a retired longshoreman, some type of heavy laborer, a guy who spent his entire life throwing bricks. He had these enormous hands, like the hands of a guy who is 6-foot-5. He was all of about 5-2. He had just had quadruple bypass surgery. He would tell jokes all the time and get everybody going. One day, he laughed so hard that he broke all the stitches in his chest and had to have another surgery. We all have these guys in our lives. Usually small in stature, but huge in character. Like a barber who has cut hair for 50 years or hotel bag man who has been on the job for decades without missing a single day. This was my kind of guy.

His story was pretty sad, but he didn't let it get to him in the least bit. His wife had already died and his son was off working on an oil rig in the North Sea. He didn't have anybody with him. But I give him credit for having a great attitude. We kind of adopted him as part of our family and my mom even bought him a pair of shorts. He had never even worn shorts in his life, but he put them right on and played it up really good. The man had the attitude of a 20-year-old and, as a result, I got really close to him.

Verna took a mid-afternoon walk each day. He took me along one day. We walked the Papworth grounds – which were expansive – until we reached the fence. It was just a short brick wall that you could see above. On the other side was The Promised Land…a pub. He had been walking here each day for the better part of a month. He told me he couldn't wait for the day to jump the fence and go have a beer or even better, bacon and eggs.

"Well, Tommy," I said. "Let's do it. Tomorrow."

So we hatched "Operation Breakout." This was roughly two weeks after my surgery. Tommy was at about the same spot since he had been re-stitched. We woke up 15 minutes before the nurses would arrive and put on our robes. Underneath I had sweatpants and Tommy had on his infamous red shorts.

His legs looked liked two chicken wings plucked clean. Mine didn't look much better, but at least they were covered by the sweatpants.

Off we went, sneaking out the side door of the ward. We made it to the fence. Now we had to get over the fence. Yes it was only about five-feet tall, but between Tommy at 5-2 and me at 5-8, we were outmatched. To top that off, I had my external pacemaker. The reason is that my resting heart rate was at about 40 beats per minute because I was in good shape. Even at death's door, I had a low resting heart rate. But that wasn't good for protocol, so they hooked me up with two wires coming directly from my heart through a hole on my side and attached to the external pacemaker.

Which was the size of a car battery.

Up to now, the pacemaker wasn't an issue. But as I faced the Papworth Wall, I had to figure this out. We surveyed and came to the conclusion to just go for it. I supported Tommy as he hiked up the wall and sat on the top. I then passed him my car battery, er, pacemaker, and he put it on top of the wall. I then jumped up. Tommy shimmied down. I passed him the pacemaker and then jumped down.

Freedom! This was *The Count of Monte Cristo*, *Papillon* and *The Great Escape* all rolled into one. We scurried across the street in our robes, car battery in tow. What a sight we must have been. Could you imagine if someone would have driven by? Just to top it all off, I later found out that Verna was 80. How awesome was this guy? We ended up having a great breakfast and a wonderful time. It was just one of those life moments that made me so happy.

As I continued to recuperate, I only had one small issue. After 10 days, I dealt with some rejection. This is very much an anticipated event as the doctors wean you off of the high doses of anti-rejection medicine until your body reacts and begins to attack this new organ. The body considers a new organ like a foreign invader. Once the doctors establish this level of rejection, they have a better idea of what kind of medicine you are going to need on a long-term basis. It was the rejection that really concerned me. I knew it was coming and although it is frightening to hear that your body is rejecting this new organ – it kind of makes you go down a dark path in your mind – I was more frustrated with the massive amounts of prednisone that they used to combat it. This made me look all puffy again, particularly in the face, and for me that was always the sign that I was sick. So looking in the mirror each day was a mental battle.

Once I got my medication at the correct level, I left it unchanged for many years. But fast-forward about seven years and I did make a dramatic change. It's a decision I feel has really helped me attain maximum heath over the past 18 years. Working with a great cardiologist, Dr. Jacques Lamothe in Las Vegas, I made the decision to begin to reduce my medicine. This was not the protocol for organ recipients. Some in the medical field might call it non-compliant, but it was far from it. Most organ recipients take their immunosuppression medicine once every 12 hours. This is necessary, in theory, to have a minimum amount in your blood stream at all times. My time of the day was clocked in at 7 a.m. and then 7 p.m. For the first seven years I took it religiously. It's a liquid that tasted like a combination of cod liver oil mixed with ammonia.

For me, however, it felt like I was becoming more and more "toxic." Me, Kelly and Dr. Lamothe huddled, and after assessing the options I ultimately chose to reduce the night dosage and then eliminate it altogether. This was highly unusual. I also reduced any other medications that I was taking down to the bare minimum. The change was risky. At any time I could have gone into massive rejection that would have almost assuredly wreaked havoc on my health. But, as I am prone to do, I had a feeling. Call it intuition or whatever, I just really have a great understanding of my body and I know when I need to get off some of this medicine. Even today when I talk to transplant surgeons, they are very surprised at my most unlikely protocol. For me it works.

The downside of all the medication I take – even after cutting it by more than half – is that I know I'm going to have kidney failure some day. I am also highly susceptible to some kinds of cancer. That's what all of these medications do. Getting an organ transplant is not a be-all, end-all solution. You are essentially trading one disease for another. I know this and recognize the challenges. All organ recipients manifest their challenges slightly differently. For me it's dehydration. I get dehydrated frequently and quickly. It was more troublesome when I was playing, particularly in the scorching heat of the desert. But even today I struggle with it. Kelly can tell instantly by looking at me if I am getting close to being dehydrated. Even before I know. She will just quietly pour me a big glass of water, watch me drink it and then without me really even noticing fill it up once, maybe twice, more. She is amazing at managing me without me even knowing it.

The other aspect of recuperating is mental. You now have someone else's body part inside you. No matter how tough or stupid I was, even I had to think this one through. Add to the fact that it was a soccer player's heart and one could obviously see it had to be worked through mentally. One of my parents told me. I can't remember which one of them told me, but they had cut out a couple of articles that day from the newspapers, which is part of how I was able to find the Fields family. I remember my parents telling me it was a young man's heart, someone who was actually younger than me and who died in an accident. I didn't get the full details of what happened until later, that he had actually died while playing soccer. The irony was something that was really hard to come to terms with.

I struggled with it for days. It wasn't weeks or months or years the way some people struggle with the mental side. The reason is that I mentioned this to Dr. Mohsin Hakim. It was actually Dr. Hakim who had performed my actual insertion surgery of the new heart under the guidance of Dr. English.

Before I get into what Dr. Hakim said, let me take a detour to talk about his amazing story. He was born in Egypt – Luxor, specifically, which is ironic given that I live in Las Vegas – to a Christian family in a mostly Muslim country. After he became a doctor, he was to be assigned to an outpost in a vast, sparsely populated part of the country because of his religious beliefs. I would imagine this was sort of like the Lestock of Egypt. Such a remote location would mean that he would be treating upset stomachs, broken bones, and headaches – very necessary to have a general practitioner who could treat anything. Mohsin had other plans and in order to achieve his goals he would have to leave his beloved family and the country he had called home.

He moved to England in order to pursue his dream of becoming a skilled surgeon and, specifically, to work on heart transplants. Upon arrival he was greeted with silence. He needed to take some tests and update his qualifications so that he was able to practice medicine in England. As he did this, time kept passing by and at one point he was forced to take a job at an obvious spot for budding thoracic surgeons.

Being a tall, slight man – maybe 5-11, 150 pounds – and looking perpetually young, I can just imagine how one of the great heart surgeons of the time was being treated like a 17-year-old as he looked at the customers and said, "Would you like original or crispy?"

Dr. Hakim eventually made his way to Papworth, where we met for the first time on an operating table on July 7th, 1986. But it was what he said to me in one of my follow-up meetings that has stayed with me and been my guiding light in all I do and how I live. Again, I was explaining how it felt weird that I had this other heart. I accepted the situation, but what I really wanted to know was how much could I really do?

Dr. Hakim looked me dead in the eye and without missing a beat he said these words;

"Simon, the idea behind heart transplantation is to live the life you lived prior to being sick."

Boom, that was a winning statement. That was all the guidance I needed. I needed someone, anyone, to tell me it was OK to go and tackle my old life again. Mohsin was the guy for me. In many ways it was more important than the actual surgery.

After I left England, I was sure I would never see Mohsin again. But life is funny that way. Just after finishing my soccer career, I spent time travelling around the country doing soccer clinics for hospitals and helping transplant programs generate publicity. One stop was the Willis Knighton Healthcare System. I was contracted by a great sports marketing company called Sportscare USA, which brought me in for a weekend. Through the organizing of the event, I learned that Dr. Hakim had moved from Papworth to the Mayo Clinic and later to start a program in Shreveport, La., at Willis Knighton. He was the top guy in charge and the program was just started, so my PR potential helped his program. I was the English-Canadian boy able to have a very cool reunion with my Egyptian surgeon in the State of Louisiana.

Talk about odd intersections. At our first dinner together (not at KFC), we caught up on our lives and I told him how he had affected me with his words. In his typically unassuming way, he deflected all the credit. Kelly and I became great friends with Mohsin, his wife Cindy and their two boys, Antony and Stefan. Tragically, Mohsin died of a cardiac arrhythmia at age 47, only eight years after I reunited with him. In 2011, 25 years after he placed a new heart in my chest, I made the trip to go and stand at his grave site, in Rochester, Minnesota, with Cindy and talk to Mohsin myself. I thanked him again for sharing the words that I attribute my attitude and long-term success to. I know he was pleased.

For years and years, Kelly kept his business card in her wallet at all times. She would call him from time to time for guidance, particularly one time when I was in an emergency situation. Even after he died, she has kept his card. At times when she has needed strength, she would look at his card and talk to him. As he did for me, Mohsin always had answers for Kelly, even from his now-lofty vantage point.

As I got closer to being discharged, I knew it would be Dr. English who made the final call. He came to see me three times after surgery. You always knew when he was coming in because the ward got a 24-hour warning. In that time, they'd make sure the floors were mopped, we all had to be in proper pajamas, all the doors were shut, the beds were made, the curtains were straight and the flowers were fresh. The odd part is that I didn't exactly get why they acted that way around him. At least I didn't back then. You understand more when you get just how important he was to what happened in England with the transplant program.

But really, he was this kind of unassuming man, a great guy who was very natural around people. When I asked to take a picture with him before I left, he was almost embarrassed to do it. He didn't want the picture taken.

As I look back on it, I know this was an ordeal that no one would want to go through. But I'm grateful that I ended up at Papworth, under the supervision of Dr. English. I'm thankful that I was turned down in Ontario. I feel like things happen for a reason and that I was meant to be at Papworth. I liked that Papworth allowed me to push the process and that the doctors and administrators were open to changing protocol. They were forward-thinking doctors led by a true leader. It was a blessing that I ended up in England.

I remember the first visit I had with Dr. Goodwin. His appointment cost something like 800 pounds, which was the rough equivalent of $1,600. That's pricey even by today's standards. But it ended up being some of the best money we spent in the whole process. Instead of running into somebody who thought he had all the answers, we ran into somebody who was willing to listen to what other people said, agree with them if they were right and come up with an aggressive plan to fix me. Then Goodwin got me to Dr. English, a man who also was willing to do what he felt was right rather than simply whatever idea got stuck in his head.

One of the odd parts is how people think about death. Most people say they're cowards, that if they're going to die they want it to happen quickly so they don't have to think about it. To me, that's not really facing the situation. It's not challenging yourself. I say that having survived, of course. But part of me knows just how close I had come to dying and I realized how much I was willing to fight to stay alive. I realized just how much will and force I had to fight for my life. I realize that when I faced death, I was able to survive long enough through sheer will and determination

Character is a funny thing. It is not something you can buy. It is not something you can artificially test. It is not something that you can measure. Character is something that is tested most when you are at your weakest. As I dodged death, I had incredible luck. I had skilled experts. I had unbelievable support. But when all of them went home and I was there fighting by myself, there was me and my character. It came down to that equation. It was the ultimate test. I hope you never have to face this test. But if you do, trust in your character.

12

RETURNING TO THE FIELD

I returned to Victoria on September 19, 1986, arriving at the Victoria International Airport to a big crowd of people waiting for me and my parents. In certain respects, it was great to see everyone. I had been gone for nearly five months and people had been following my story in the news, so I know there was a lot of curiosity about me.

In other respects, it was the start of being in this fish-bowl kind of existence. For my mom, I think it helped her a lot to immediately reconnect with people and share all the news. It was a way for her to get rid of some of the anguish and sorrow. It was a triumph in a way, especially after everything we had been through. This was almost two years removed from when I got sick in the winter of 1984-85.

The homecoming was fine, but not really my style. I preferred to fly under the radar, but it became clear almost immediately that this was just not going to be an option. I figured I would go right back to the University of Victoria and start taking classes again. The more I thought about it, I decided to wait until January. I wanted to get my strength back. So I would be in the weight room every day and I would run every day. Compared to what you would expect somebody with a heart transplant to be doing, I was probably off the charts.

And people couldn't quite get that. When I first returned, I had been given all these memberships to different health clubs and things like that. People were being nice and doing what they could to support "The Heart

Guy." Most viewed it as a curiosity. For me, it was like people at the zoo going to see the monkey ... except I was the monkey. It was like, "Oh, let's see The Heart Guy work out." I understood, but the problem was that I couldn't really work out the way I needed to for being an athlete again. When you go to these nice, chic gyms, like Bally's or L.A. Fitness, everybody has the nice workout clothes and the outfits and they're definitely trying to get healthy and do all the right things.

But that's not how an athlete works out. It didn't work for me at all. I would go two or three times and realize it was not for me. When an athlete works out, it's a whole different level. It's about getting drenched with sweat to the point that no one other than another athlete would ever want to be around you. Seriously, when you're an athlete playing at that high a level, you're on the exercise bike for 30 minutes, going as fast as you can. You can't do that in a public place with a bunch of regular people around because you look ridiculous. People think you're crazy and, to a certain extent, you are.

So I ended up going to a lot of these, shall we say, smaller, more intimate and maybe not as new gyms. It's like the places where you see the old-time boxers work. There are no frills. You want to be there to work, not to look pretty. Great coaches talk about that stuff all the time. When professional teams get fancy equipment and new training facilities, you often hear the coaches and trainers grumble, "This ain't the kind of place that makes you tough."

I used two places. One was the YMCA in downtown Victoria. At the time it was old. Seriously old. There's no way around it, old and beat up. The second was the Gordon Head Recreation Center. It was just down from my house. The names aren't important, but you should immediately get an idea of what they look like.

Working out is important because it's all about what you're willing to sacrifice. Being at some pretty gym doesn't work with the adage, "It's not what you do when people are watching, it's what you do when people aren't watching." One day, I was at the Gordon Head Rec Center. The workout room was maybe 20 feet by 20 feet, the size of a large bedroom. I'm sure it's different now, but back then the weights were old. The exercise bike was old. The treadmill was old. The place was not air-conditioned. Literally, and figuratively, it stunk.

I immediately fell in love with the place.

For some reason, on this particular day, this girl who knew my brother was there, too. We weren't talking or anything, but I was in there and I was really pushing my body as hard as I could. The sweat was just pouring off me as I rode the bike and I was going and going and going. A couple of days later, my brother called me and said he ran into that girl and she said, "Simon is absolutely nuts." I am sure she was right on with her assessment.

In the first few months after I had my transplant and returned home, my mom sent me to a transplant support group meeting in Vancouver. It was a bunch of people, mostly guys, who had transplants and were dealing with their recovery or whatever else was going on. To be honest, I thought there were all weasels back then when I was younger. I called them "The Weasel Group" because they were all sitting around, obsessed with their transplant. Look, I was 21, super-opinionated and I knew right away that this attitude didn't work for me. I used to get in trouble with my mom all the time for saying that, but it's really how I felt. I thought a lot of these guys were wrapped up in being transplants recipients. They acted like victims, sniffing around for people to feel sorry for them. I couldn't handle that way of thinking.

I remember distinctly sitting next to one guy during one of the meetings and I asked him how long ago he had his transplant. So he tells me, "Eighteen months ago and I'm going back to work tomorrow." Are you serious, 18 months? At that point, I was three months removed from my transplant and I was lifting weights and training to play soccer again. This guy is taking six times as long as me and just getting back to work. I understand my situation was special. I was young, I was fit, I received the heart of a young man who was also fit. I get it, but still, I just kept shaking my head at how much time this guy wasted in his life just trying to get back to it.

My thinking has matured since then and I am much more understanding of the challenges associated with transplantation. Nonetheless, I have noticed a big flaw in the recovery process of organ recipients. The system is setup to keep the recipient in a perpetual state of disability.

Let me explain.

By definition, an organ transplant is life saving in practically every situation. The patient has been given a second chance at life with this procedure. The recipient is labeled all kinds of things: A miracle, amazing and brave are just a few of the words. I was "The Heart Guy." Those around the patient – his friends, his family and maybe his co-workers – tell him how brave he is. They all heap on positive attention.

Then there are the doctors and the follow-up care. Yes, it is important to follow the regimen of visits and medication, but it is very easy to become obsessed with it. Take your pills. Test your blood. Monthly checks. Educate yourself. Go to this doctor. Go to that doctor. It can suck you in and before you know it, you can't get out of surrounding yourself with doctors and medical staff who see you as a "patient" and your friends and family who see you as "a miracle." It's human nature that this type of attention is almost always embraced. It's almost always positive feedback and soon you allow yourself to become this quasi-caricature of yourself.

I have seen this literally hundreds, if not thousands, of times. For me it is, and always will be, counterproductive to the goals that I have set in life. I don't want to be viewed as "The Heart Guy" and become a caricature of myself. I feel that so strongly that I will run away from the attention.

Too many people misunderstand how they should handle getting a transplant. A transplant is an opportunity to go back to your life. Obviously, if some of that life is unhealthy, you have to change it. Whether that's eating too much or smoking or whatever destructive thing that may have contributed to you being there in the first place, who have to end that behavior. But whatever your hope and dream was before you got your surgery, that should be your hope and dream now. That's how I look at it. I just keep coming back again and again to what Dr. Hakim said to me, that the goal of the surgery was for me to go back to my life.

For too many people, the transplant becomes their life. My utter disdain for being "The Heart Guy" allowed me to get back to my life, especially when it came to playing soccer again. I didn't want to be considered different in the context of my sport. Once I started playing, the other players weren't going to give a crap about my condition when we were on the field. It's not like they were going to get out of my way and let me score. They didn't care. They had a job to do, whether it was to keep a scholarship or actually get paid.

In fact, to a certain extent, I was going to get tested athletically more because of my transplant. That's how I figured. Some people might look at this as cruel, but it's reality. If you think your opponent is hurting or can't handle something, you're going to test him. You're going to push that button, whether it's physical or mental, and keep pushing it. I knew that was coming and I welcomed it because that was going to make me the best player I could be. Sometimes this can be really troubling, like in the 2006 World Cup final, when Zinedine Zidane of France head-butted Italy's Marco Materazzi and got ejected.

It's one of the most famous moments in soccer history. Zidane was the best player in the world at that moment. He was awarded the Golden Ball as the best player at the World Cup that year, but he lost his composure and got kicked out at a critical time. Why? Materazzi insulted him. The official story is that Materazzi said something about Zidane's sister. I'm sure there was more than that leading up to the headbutt and years later Zidane said he "would rather die" than apologize to Materazzi, so it was probably really building up. But the point is that when you're playing a sport at that level, you're going to get pushed to your limits. Sometimes it's disgusting and unsportsmanlike, stuff you would never dream of doing yourself, but it still happens and you have to be mentally prepared for it.

For me, I was ready to be pushed. I knew that I was going to get kicked or hit or any of the other things that happen all the time in soccer. I was probably going to get more of it as people tried to figure out if I could handle it. My attitude was, bring it on. Let's go, push me. The attitude I saw when I went to the transplant support group was just the opposite.

Of course, that was one of the best things about soccer in terms of my recovery. I was already different. I was a prominent soccer player. I was on the road to fulfilling my dreams. I had had a chance to play in the World Cup, even if it evaporated. I was already really proud of what I had become. I just wanted to get back to it. For me, the transplant made it so I could do that, but my previous achievements were gone in some ways because of how people viewed me. I used to see stories on television or in the newspaper that basically said "Transplant Guy Does This" like it was some big deal. The story even could have been about me.

Over the 25 years since my transplant, I've become far more understanding of what I'm trying to say. Too often, I came off as too harsh with people and I get that with the advantage of hindsight. I don't fault people for being scared. I don't fault them for that feeling of recognition or support they get from going through this. It's all valid, but it's not really what this great gift of medical science is trying to achieve.

Really, what people should do after they get a transplant is push harder to achieve the things they want. I know people who ran marathons after having a transplant and I knew that as good an athlete as I was, I was never in the kind of shape to do that. If you have the chance for a longer life with a transplant, don't waste it. Do those things you dreamed of, that you always believed you could do or always wanted to do.

Along the same lines, I don't think I was what you would call "grateful" the way so many would have expected. I was certainly happy to be alive, but I wasn't sitting around thinking about all the things that I was happy to have. I think that's a matter of being young and trying to be both mentally and physically tough. Some of it is that you don't really have the perspective at 21 to know what you truly could have lost. I didn't have my children and I hadn't met Kelly yet. I hadn't had the life experiences that I was about to have. I didn't know what I could have missed and the joy (and even sorrow) that life was going to bring to me.

I didn't sit around and say, "Man, what a lucky guy I am." I didn't think about all the things that could have gone wrong, how I might have died and not had my life. Back then, at least in my view, if you start thinking about life that way, all the bad things do start to happen. I'm about living life at 100 percent full speed and that's how I approached it from the minute I got out of surgery. That's how I lived it before the surgery and I was intent on returning to my life as it was. That is what Dr. Hakim had reinforced in me after my surgery.

The great part about returning to Victoria was that so many people cared about me.

The bad part about returning to Victoria was that so many people cared about me.

This is what I started off trying to say with the "fish-bowl" effect. I was obviously very well known around town because so many people worked so hard to help me. My friends like Tak, Ian Klitsie and the McAdams family, they were just the tip of the iceberg. It was humbling to realize how many people had worked so hard to help, who cared that deeply about whether I survived. At the same time, it got overwhelming.

There was this routine I went through it. I wish I had a dollar for every time it happened. I wouldn't have ever had to work if I had just made that money. Someone would come up to me and ask, "How are you doing?" Not, "How ya doin'?" in some informal fashion. It was more of a probing question. I would say, "I'm fine." Then they'd tilt their head, get a little more poignant and say, "No, how *are* you doing?" Again, "I'm fine." Everybody was looking for some deep, philosophical answer, as if I was scared and they could somehow lift my burden.

The questions went on in some derivation of that original theme. Could I do this? Yes. Could I do that? Yes. Could I walk and chew gum at the same time? Oh, I'm not sure about that one. Look, I try not to be really sarcastic about this stuff, but it really got to be overbearing. It was like eight or 12 weeks after my surgery and there were reporters and cameramen outside my house waiting for days on end for me to go on a run so they could follow me around. There was no peace and no privacy. Basically, I became known as "The Heart Guy." It was like being the bubble boy.

Most people treated me with kid gloves, as if I was suddenly different, this precious piece of china that could break at any moment. It took me a long time to overcome that. Really, it took me moving away. The issue was that everybody seemed to feel that because maybe they had helped me out that they were now entitled to tell me how I should live. I would go out with my friends to a restaurant and order a burger and some fries. Literally, every time I did that, some older woman who looked like she could be my grandmother would walk up to me and ask, rhetorically, "Should you really be eating that?" Then they'd put $5 on the table, "God bless you" and walk away. When I say that it happened 150 times, I'm totally serious.

I wanted to scream, "My problem was not clogged arteries!!!!!!!!" My problem was that a virus had destroyed my heart. I hadn't destroyed it through irresponsible eating habits. Yeah, maybe I pushed myself at times, but it wasn't that I was eating a pound of bacon with a side of lard every day.

Playing sports was the same way. When I started to play soccer again, the guys on my team wouldn't touch me at first during practice. It was like they were afraid I would fall over and maybe die on the field. The only way those guys got over that was when I started getting stuck in and being physical with them. It took that for them to feel OK about competing against me again.

I remember in the couple of years immediately after I had the operation, it felt almost as if I was talking about myself in third person. There was this other guy who had all these problems. And then there was me. I wasn't that guy anymore and I didn't want to think about myself that way. That way of thinking was counter-productive to what I wanted to do. When Kelly and I started going out, she didn't know anything about my story, which was great. Then I let her in on everything that happened so that she would understand. She started reading all these transcripts of interviews I had done and she would say: "This is not you. I don't understand it, it doesn't seem like you."

It wasn't that I changed so much after the surgery. Yes, my focus on what I wanted to be became stronger, but it wasn't as if I went from being some overweight, do-nothing, aimless person to saying I wanted to become a marathon runner. I went back to being what I had intended to do before the surgery. The time when I changed was during the 18 months I was sick. That's when I was a different person. When I got my transplant I went back to being the person I was before. During those 18 months, I wasn't the nicest person I could be. I wasn't thinking beyond myself because I was so unhealthy. That's different from my normal self.

The point is that I didn't have a negative experience with the heart transplant personally. The transplant was the thing that made me better. Yeah, there were some minor inconveniences, like getting tests. I might have to spend a day at the doctor every six months or year that other people don't have to spend. Big deal. That's the price you pay to have the life you want.

When it came time to return to the University of Victoria and the program, I had to go through this long list of tests. It was test after test as the doctors sought to determine if I was fit enough to return to soccer. Some of it got a little irritating because I knew full well I could play, but the doctors were being unbelievably cautious.

The other problem I had was a lot of bad memories from the previous couple of years of playing at the University of Victoria. I remembered always being cold, just physically never feeling right, and the school's field can be one of the coldest places around come fall. When it's raining at 4:30 in the afternoon on a cold November day, it's just miserable and I didn't want to do that again.

I also started to realize as time went on that the university didn't really want me to play again. It was a mutual thing at a certain point because I think too many people there were worried that something was going to go wrong and I would die. There was already this attitude out there among a lot of people that I shouldn't be eating hamburgers and fries. Do you really think there were people who thought it was a good idea for me to play soccer again? Seriously, everybody had an opinion about how I should run my life and most of those opinions were negative about the idea.

As time went on, the athletic director at the university, this really good guy named Ken Shields, basically told me that they weren't going to let me play. I knew Shields wasn't playing games with me because he was a coach like my dad, and a highly respected one at that. He was basically the greatest college basketball coach in Canadian history. He won nine Canadian Interuniversity Sport men's basketball titles at Victoria and retired with the most victories in CIS history. He coached the Canadian National team, won the country's James Naismith Award and is even in the Canadian Basketball Hall of Fame.

So when you're talking to a guy like that, you're not talking to some bureaucrat who's just trying to cover his ass. Shields knew the lay of the land and how people really felt. At that point, it's not that I wasn't welcome, but my future there was seriously limited because of how people viewed me, and that was frustrating. It's sort of like how family friend Ian Bridge, my idol when I was coming up and now a respected former player and coach, put it:

"Victoria is a soccer town and Simon was part of a soccer family and community. His dad Dave was very much a strong influence in my career, like a coach and mentor. When Simon had the heart problem, it was like this was such a big loss for the game because this was a big talent. He had the most skill of the three brothers. When he came back and able to play again, it was kind of you really didn't notice his talent, it was more of this is the kid with somebody else's heart. He still had more talent than everybody talked about, (but) I think the transplant news story became more for the people in the media, the sports media, to write about. Back at that time to write about soccer was not that glamorous of a thing. (With Simon) it was more of a human-interest story.

"I can see that (being a problem). Sometimes when you are coming back from an injury, the press just wants to talk about those kind of things. 'How does your knee feel? What is it like to have a heart transplant?' I'm sure he just wanted to talk about his ability as a player. Once you have a heart transplant, you have to deal with it, so you probably don't want to discuss everything. You just want to get on with playing soccer. I can see how that would have been frustrating for him. I think his special talent that I can remember was a real, kind of explosive first three strides. The ball didn't slow down, and he also had a quick soccer brain … that's someone that solves problems on the fly very quickly in the game, whether it's the defensive side of the game or the offensive side of the game. You see solutions naturally, understand where to go, where to be, where to pass. It's something that you don't necessarily learn but it is in you. Coming from a soccer family, I knew Simon would always be very much more explosive than any other kids at an early age. His dad was a great coach, his brothers all played. His mom was a great supporter of the kids, so I just think he came from an environment that nurtured that soccer brain."

My problem was that I wanted to use my soccer brain again and people weren't letting me do that. I didn't want to be a human-interest story. I wanted to compete. I didn't want to be defined by other people's definition of what I should or shouldn't do. Yes, there was risk involved in playing. How much exactly? I have no idea because I wasn't thinking about it that way. I was thinking about playing.

The other thing is that people don't understand that just living isn't always what you want to do. It's like Robert Fields said when we met in England. He was so happy that I didn't just get this heart and sit around watching television. He was overjoyed by the fact I had taken this opportunity and made the most out of it. Yes, maybe I could have died playing soccer. I know my parents thought about that and I know my mother had to deal with people second-guessing her for allowing me to play. What those people never understood is that I wouldn't have become the same person if I hadn't tried. I could have played it safe and done nothing with my life and I might have still died. Or I could take a chance and risk dying doing something that made me feel happy and satisfied.

To me, that's not even a choice. If I was ever going to get a chance to do more than run some clinics, become a coach and trade on my fame as "The Heart Guy," I was going to have to leave my hometown.

I hate to say it that way, but this is how I felt at the time. I felt like I was forced out of my hometown by the perceptions of other people. I was simply over loved by Victoria. I had to find a place to go where people weren't going to look at me this way, a place where someone was willing to take a risk. It also wouldn't hurt me to go somewhere that was a lot warmer and easier for me to play.

What better place than Las Vegas?

13

Viva Las Vegas

By the early part of 1987, it was pretty clear to me that I was done playing soccer in Victoria and that it was time for a change of scenery from the Garden City. If it is possible for a city to love and care for someone too much, I was it. It is something that I struggled with then and I have continued to struggle with. I knew in my heart the love and compassion the residents of this idyllic city had for me. At the same time, it was really affecting me. There was simply too much pressure on me, from attempting a comeback in soccer to hanging out with my buddies to what I ate and even what I drank. I would have been a prisoner of other people's judgment. It seemed, whether real or not, that no matter what I did, if I stayed in Victoria I would always be known as "The Heart Guy." This just simply wasn't going to work for me.

That spring, I had practiced a little bit with the University of Victoria. But for some reason, I just knew it wasn't right. We had our annual road trip coming up, so it would be a good time to think things through. Each year for the past three or four years since I started college (with the exception of when I was busy in England with that whole transplant issue), five of us would head down the West Coast of the United States. Our group was me, Brad McAdams, Clay Crust (the prankster of the group), Wade Loukes (a basketball player at UVic) and Darryl Montgomery (a hockey-playing buddy from high school).

We would follow the Interstate 5 south, making detours at ballparks along the way. From the Kingdome in Seattle to Candlestick Park in San Francisco to the Oakland Coliseum to Dodger Stadium in L.A. or The Big A in Anaheim. We just drove, laughed, drank beer and generally had a good time. The fact we were driving the Loukes family van didn't seem to bother us in the slightest. Actually, it wasn't really a "family" van. It just belonged to his family. It was a cargo van with only two seats, so three of us had to sit in the back on a mattress and relax while two took turns driving while listening to the one cassette tape we had. Yeah, it was Hall & Oates. Ridiculous.

This particular year, we were in rare form. After leaving Seattle, we drove south and made it just to Redbluff, Calif., just south of the Oregon border. It was home to a Champion outlet store that Loukes loved. So we stayed that night in one of those generic, two-story motels that you find adjoining highways everywhere in America. Rooms go for about $39 a night and sometimes you feel like that is overcharging.

Along the way that night, we met a few of Redbluff's finest young ladies, drunk a few beers, and were being basic, rambunctious, college kids. No big deal and nothing stupid happened, at least that we can remember.

We were awakened the next day to the sound of thumping on the door of our motel room door. "Police! Open up!"

What the heck? We groggily look around and notice that Crust and Montgomery aren't in the room. That wasn't unusual, sometimes one or two of us would stay in the van while others slept in the motel. So automatically we yell back -- and let's agree for the sake of decorum that we yelled, "Bug off."

More pounding.

"Open up!! It's the police!!"

"Bug off, Clay."

"Open up!!! It's the Redbluff Police!!!"

"Whatever Clay! Bug off!"

"You have 10 seconds to open this door! It's the Redbluff Police!"

So I struggle to my feet and open the door and see two strapping Redbluff policemen dressed in very intimidating-type uniforms. I can only imagine what they see. Three young guys, beer cans everywhere, maybe a couple girls (maybe not, I'm not gonna say) and I am sure we look like death.

One of the officers said, "Can you step outside please?"

Now a little nervous, but not terribly because we know we kept the fun to ourselves, the three of us complied. As we stand on the balcony overlooking the parking lot, the mystery starts to reveal itself. What we see is that someone had taken one of those foam fire extinguishers and "foamed" every car in the parking lot. There must have been 30 cars, all foamed from top to bottom.

With the exception of one vehicle … our van. It was spotless, not a drop of foam on it. Whoever the "foam vandal" was must have had great respect for our travel plans. Way to go Crust. It didn't take Sherlock freaking Holmes to figure this one out.

We were given two options: Spend a night in jail or pay $300 and be escorted out of town. We enjoyed the fine escort services of the Redbluff Police.

Steadily heading south, we get to Los Angeles. This year we are making a detour. Adam had agreed to play for UNLV and was already enrolled. Off we headed to Sin City.

We got to UNLV and it was 95 degrees. Immediately, I loved it. Being in the cold in Victoria that winter was a big reminder to me about how bad I felt before the surgery. It wasn't nearly as bad, but the cold just wasn't working for me. Now, I'm in Las Vegas and it's hot. Not only that, but my brother was living large. He had this great apartment with a pool, a whirlpool, a weight room, free beer and girls everywhere. It seemed like a perfect escape for me.

More important, there was an opportunity. Adam was playing soccer at UNLV for Coach Barry Barto. Now, the short story to this is that Adam talked to Barto, knowing that the team needed a forward who could score. He told Barto that he had a brother who was pretty good and could help the team….but that, by the way, I had just had a heart transplant. Barto, for whatever reason, agreed to have a look at me. So a "scrimmage" was set up.

My preparation for the scrimmage had been watching ball games, drinking beer with the guys and generally carousing. Perfect.

At the scrimmage, it was just one of those days. For some reason, almost everything I did turned out right. I scored goals. I took guys on and torched them. Each touch was as good as the next. I had stamina for days (something that later in my career I struggled with) and I played at a level that was frankly above the guys I was playing with. It was as good a tryout as I could have had.

At this point, I had two years of eligibility left and because I had sat out last season at Victoria after the heart surgery, I was eligible to transfer and play right away. Barto approached me after the session and said something to the effect of: "You're a pretty good player. You've had a heart transplant. You're not going to die on me, are you?" I give Barto a lot of credit. It was a fair question and he got right to the point.

In my usual smart-ass way, I said, "Well, if I die, I die. But I promise you, I won't." He could tell, even in my flippant way that I was serious, so he worked on getting permission and the paperwork done. Then he said, "How am I supposed to feel if you die out there?" I just said, "It's my choice, not yours. I want to do this."

"I looked at it more as an opportunity to give someone a new life," Barto said. "You could see and hear in his personality that is was something he really wanted to do. If we could provide an opportunity, he was going to give us his all. My biggest concern was how would I feel if he dropped dead? His response was like, 'If that's what's meant to be, that's what's meant to be.' "

Of course, there's a little longer back story to my returning to play. Barto had to run the idea of my playing past the administration at UNLV, which was surprisingly open to the idea of allowing a heart transplant recipient to compete. Of course, we had to jump through some hoops to deal with any liability the school may have faced if anything happened. Barto met with Dr. Brad Rothermel, the UNLV athletic director. Rothermel is the man credited with putting UNLV on the athletic map and in the minds of the American public. He was the AD for 11 years and was instrumental in building UNLV athletics. He had vision and poise. Luckily for me, he took chances on people that some might not. After Barto explained to Rothermel my very unique situation, the AD went about working the back channels, meeting with as many people as needed, including the UNLV President Robert Maxson to get approval for me to play. Along the way, doctors and lawyers had to weigh in.

"Probably most (school administrators) might have shied away from it, but Simon would rather have done it and failed than not have tried, and there's something very special to that type of attitude," Rothermel said. "Simon is a great hustler, an exemplary person as an athlete and in the classroom. That's the type of person you fight for."

Rothermel kept asking the doctors if they thought I was healthy enough to play and they asked the lawyers about the liability. They talked to my doctors back home and got reports from the doctors back in England. Along the way, everyone involved was apprehensive but seemed willing to give me the chance as long as they and the school were covered from a liability standpoint. Liability became a subplot to my career. It was as if people would say, "Yes, Simon you can play, but you need to sign this and this … and this … and this … oh, and this one … and that one."

You get the idea.

As I look back on it, I have remained friends with many of those early UNLV administrators. Jerry Koloskie, in particular, makes me chuckle every time I see him. Koloskie is now the number two guy in the UNLV athletic department. At the time I played he was the head athletic trainer. Could you imagine the first time he heard that the next student-athlete he would be responsible for was a heart transplant recipient who had a pacemaker? And, oh yeah, he will be playing the very physical sport of soccer, in temperatures close to 115 degrees. I'm not sure if there is an athletic training class for that one.

I was also fortunate in another way. In March 1990, almost three years after I started the process with UNLV, Hank Gathers of Loyola Marymount University in Los Angeles collapsed and died during a college basketball game. I remember watching the news that day. As I watched Gathers stumble on the court, I actually physically slumped down in my chair when I saw it. It was a terrible tragedy and it hit me more than anything in my life had before. I was hoping that no one would put me and Hank together in any news stories. I knew this tragedy could mean the end of my career if people put us together. Yes it was selfish, but this was the stigma I knew I was living with. I didn't have *any* room for any mistakes in terms of health issues.

Gathers is thought to have died because he stopped taking his heart medicine (he had been diagnosed with the problem a few months earlier). His family still ended up filing a negligence suit for $30 million and settled for $2.4 million.

If Gathers had passed away prior to me getting to UNLV, there's no way I would have gotten a chance to play. Never. The lawyers would have come in and said, "Heck no, that's a crazy idea." There probably weren't enough legal waivers you could write up and sign to get past that situation.

Particularly when you consider the other maneuver I had to pull to get permission to play. I was in very strange situation. I was still technically a student-athlete affiliated with the University of Victoria. Now I wanted to play for UNLV. UNLV asked me to go to UVic for permission to transfer and to prove that I was eligible to play in Canada. Problem was, I knew that I wasn't eligible to play in Canada.

I had already had some preliminary conversations with Ken Shields, the hall of fame basketball coach and UVic athletic director, about my future and my possibility of playing. Shields is a not only a hall of fame coach but also a hall of fame guy. When we met he was direct, sincere and, although he understood my desire to play, he was not quite in the same situation as the guys in UNLV. The administrators at UVic were much more knowledgeable about my story. Both the good and the bad. They considered me "The Heart Guy" from the news and this worked against Shields' ability to get me clearance to play.

So Shields and I had to work out a little deal. I knew I couldn't play at UVic because of both the public pressure and the internal university pressure. Shields agreed to say that I was eligible to play at UVic as long as I swore to him that I wasn't going to use it against him later to actually play at UVic again. I give Shields a lot of credit. Other administrators probably would have told me to go to hell, figuring that in the worst-case scenario, in which I die, they're going to be held responsible for my death somehow. But Shields knew what this meant to me. He knew what it was to be an athlete with a burning desire to play and he did everything he could to help me, even if that included a little blurring of the facts.

So I got my letter from UVic indicating I was eligible to play in Canada. From there, Rothermel did the paperwork and got all the permissions. As I look back on the process, the open attitudes of Shields, Rothermel and Barto were the key. Really, to me, Barto was critical because he was the perfect match for me in terms of mindset.

In 1982, Barto had left a cozy job as coach and administrator at Philadelphia University (also known as Philadelphia Textile) in Pennsylvania. At the time, soccer in America was still largely an East Coast sport played primarily at the upper-crust private high schools and small colleges. Some of the schools like North Carolina and Virginia had developed strong programs, but it was extremely regionalized.

The western part of the United States was a soccer wasteland. Barto came to UNLV to basically create the program from scratch. He was charged with making UNLV a relevant, national program. In that way, Barto was my kind of guy; a risk-taker with big goals. As my brother Adam said, "Barto could have coached the rest of his career at Philadelphia and lived a comfortable life."

Barto had a strong background in the game dating to the 1960s, back when soccer was barely on the radar of American sports. He had attended Philadelphia University and then went on to play as a midfielder in the North American Soccer League for teams like the Montreal Olympique, the Philadelphia Atoms and the Fort Lauderdale Strikers. He also played for the U.S. national team in the 1970s and was the captain for two years. In the soccer world, Barto was a *player*.

The other thing I loved about Barto was his uncomplicated approach to my heart transplant. He didn't think about a lot of other issues and concern himself with how he might be perceived. Of course, it helped that I was largely unknown in Las Vegas. Plus, the UNLV basketball team was a much bigger deal, so it's not like anybody was going to spend night and day concerned with some soccer player. Barto treated me like any other student-athlete and that is all I had been looking for.

"To me, Simon's whole attitude was refreshing and it set a standard for him with teammates," Barto said. "I don't think they understood it completely, but they could see it. Everyone knew what he had been through and the challenges he faced on a daily basis just to play soccer. They saw how important it was to him and I think people looked at each other and said, 'If he can be out there, we should be able to do at least what we're being asked to do.

"The way he trained so hard, it made everybody better, mentally and physically. He was relentless and he did it in a way that was natural. Yeah, he was a little cocky, but not in a 'I'm going to show up everybody else type of way.' It was a way that drew people in, not drove them away ... I believe he was a very gifted player from a talent standpoint, but the mental aspect of going out and doing it all the time is what separated him from the rest. There are a lot of talented players who don't work very hard. He's the talented guy who works his butt off and he shared that energy with everybody else.

"If you're looking for the model student-athlete, who you want to have represent the school and be the face of your program both on the field and off it, Simon is that guy. He has the respect and the leadership. Whatever the model is, he fits the model. You don't get many players in your career who are like that."

That praise means a lot to me, even all these years later. I finally arrived in Las Vegas on Aug. 15, 1987, three months after I had originally had my tryout. I was about two weeks late for preseason training because I had to work at some soccer camps and finish some obligations in Victoria. Then, it took a while for UVic to finalize all the paperwork for my transfer. By the time it all got taken care of, I missed the first three games of the season. As frustrating as that was, I didn't mind. I just felt like I was on such a different path by then. Between the weather, the new surroundings and the smell of opportunity in the air, I knew I had made the right choice for me at the time.

Most important, I wasn't "The Heart Guy" anymore.

One of the things I asked UNLV was that I wanted to defray as much publicity as I could about my transplant. There were a couple of stories that came out when I first got there, but nothing too big. I told the sports information people with UNLV, "Just tell the media that I'm not interested in talking about it." They did and the media left me alone. I was able to, in a sense, hide for a couple of years. I could wear shorts and tee shirts, go to class and hang out with the guys from the team. I could enjoy life and be anonymous, which was such a relief.

I never had some grand plan to live in Las Vegas for the rest of my life. I just knew that it was the right place at that time for me. It was a golden two years when I went to UNLV. Everything was (and still is) great about Las Vegas. I don't have a bad word I can say about how it has gone, especially my initial experience. Eventually, people found out about my story even though I never offered to talk about it. I wasn't keeping it some secret or anything like that. But people were curious. The good news was that the attention wasn't nearly the same. Las Vegas was and is a basketball town. Probably always will be. The Runnin' Rebels dominated the sports pages. Whether we liked it or not, it allowed the other sports, like soccer, to remain in the shadows. It was ideal for me.

In the spring of 1987, just as I got to Las Vegas for that little scrimmage that Barto ran, the basketball team had just finished a 37-2 season and had made the National Collegiate Athletic Association Final Four, losing to Indiana in the semifinals in a stunner. In 1990, the year after I got out of UNLV, the basketball team went 35-5 and won the national championship for the first and only time, kicking Duke's ass in the title game with this amazing team that had three eventual first-round draft picks (Larry Johnson, who was the No. 1 overall pick in 1991, Stacey Augmon and Greg Anthony). While I was a student at UNLV, the Thomas and Mack Center rocked on Maryland Parkway. UNLV basketball was becoming America's favorite (or hated, depending on your perspective) team under the direction of Las Vegas' most famous resident, coach Jerry Tarkanian. It was like nothing a kid from a stoic, British-flavored city like Victoria had ever seen before. Like most others, the light shows, Tark the Shark, and the 18,500 people in the famous Thomas & Mack Center every night, the whole thing took my breath away.

One of my jobs I had while at UNLV was working in the equipment room. Being Canadian and not eligible to work off campus, it was a perfect job for me. Most of the time, I would just fold towels, hand out uniforms, do a little laundry and get paid a little bit. It was a classic equipment room with everything from football helmets to baseball gloves to volleyball nets and everything in between. However, the size and scope of the operation was new to me. When the basketball players would show up, they'd come in, knock on the cage where all the equipment was kept and say, "Hey, I need some new shoes." They went through a pair of shoes like every three games during the season or every two weeks in the offseason. And we're talking about shoes that went for like $110 a pair in the store. For me at the time, it made quite an impression. I decided to calculate how many pairs the 12-member team went through that year. It ended up being 272 pairs of top-of-the-line Nikes. This was a lot different than what I was used to.

The benefits of playing at a school like UNLV with its enormous basketball success was the overflow the soccer program enjoyed. Even though the basketball team got the attention, everything they did for the soccer team was first-class. We stayed in four- and five-star hotels with nice suites, nice brunches, travel gear and great support. Walking into the Newport Beach Marriott in Los Angeles in October when it was 85 degrees, preparing to play UCLA, is much different than visiting Lethbridge, Alberta in October with below-freezing temperatures. This was not the same game that I was brought up on. The difference between rainy and cold UVic and palm tree-lined, sun-drenched Southern California was about as opposite as one could get. It was heaven for me.

The quality of the college game in the United States was beginning to improve. The United States was moving towards a more focused approach related to its national team and the college game was becoming the place for elite players to develop their games. This has since changed where players are now encouraged to join academies. But, at the time, the college game was the single biggest breeding ground for the U.S. National Team talent. In my college career, I played against some of the very best U.S. National Team players in history, including Kasey Keller, Cobi Jones, Eric Wynalda, John Harkes and Tony Meola, UNLV was a bit different. Barto recognized that he probably wasn't going to get the very best East Coast or West Coast players. Although he got a few very good ones, UNLV soccer was only just beginning to get on the soccer map. The 1984-86 UNLV teams really created a platform for the program, so I arrived just at the right time to enjoy their success and have some of my own.

In terms of playing, I performed well. I did struggle with one unique issue, however. As part of my surgery, I had a pacemaker implanted just below my ribcage. Again, the reasoning was that I had an extremely low resting heart rate. As a kid trying to keep up with two older brothers, I had developed an extraordinary stamina over the years and just was blessed with a low resting heart rate (about 40 to 45 beats per minute). After surgery the doctors in England were not comfortable with this low of a rate, so they implanted the first of about 10 pacemakers I have had since. The first however was the most troublesome. It was set so that my rate could never go below 60 beats per minute. There was no heart-rate limit at the high end, so playing was never a problem. Resting was the problem.

Each night I would go to sleep and inevitably my heart rate would drop below 60. The amplitude of the pacemaker made it so that when it engaged and took over from my natural rhythm, it would cause a small sensation just below my ribs. Almost like a centralized and powerful hiccup. Well, at 2 a.m., it would be an understatement to say that this was slightly annoying. As soon as the pacemaker kicked in the middle of the night, I would have to get up and start doing jumping jacks, or running in place to get my heart rate back over 60 so I could get some more rest. My brother Adam, who was my roommate by then (when he was actually there), found this all very amusing. Me, not so much.

Aside from my unique circumstances, the teams I played on at UNLV were also unique. Barto recruited certain types of players. I think he built teams – certainly the teams I played for – not just on talent, but on character. Chemistry was huge and he was a master at putting people together in training, in classes and in living arrangements.

The way it worked is that almost everybody on the team was from somewhere else. They had moved to Las Vegas to go to school. Barto would room four guys together in a two-bedroom apartment. There were like eight guys living in two apartments in one complex and eight guys living in two apartments in another complex really close by. When we went out, everybody ran together. It could be to play basketball or tennis or hit the clubs. It was always the soccer players hanging together. This is not unusual, but there was one difference: We were in Vegas. We'd head down to the Vegas Strip every once in awhile. We'd hit the Gold Coast for the 99-cent breakfast at 5 a.m. after a night out at the pub. Or after a night at Carlos Murphys, stumble back home to continue with a keg party until the sun came up. There were a lot of typical fraternity-and-sorority-type parties with the college girls. Nothing too crazy and mostly we bonded as a team. This part of the game, in my experience, is the same in any part of the world. The relationships that you build while playing a sport are far and away more important than the game itself. This time at UNLV delivered lifelong relationships for me, including my first UNLV college roommate Doug Borgel, who is now my son's High School Coach at Bishop Gorman High School.

As for the academics, I had to make up for the time I'd lost from my surgery and going through rehabilitation. For some reason, and for the first time in my life, I really thrived as it related to grades. I was still a Physical Education major, taking a lot of education courses because I still figured I was going to be a teacher and coach. Along with getting stronger, and enjoying the party side of college life, I focused on my academics. I was able to be extremely successful academically and started to build my confidence in that regard. That said, all of this paled in comparison to what I really found in my two years in Las Vegas: After being sick for a few years, I was able to resume my relationship with my brother.

Being around Adam again was fantastic. Adam is as happy of an individual as you can find. He will talk to anybody, anytime and for any reason. He is the perfect counterbalance to me. I'm naturally shy and more reserved. Like me, he has stayed in Las Vegas and made his home with his beautiful wife Jill and three kids (Kyleigh, Coleman and Keegan) here, so we're together a lot. Adam got into UNLV after an All-American campaign playing junior college soccer in California.

Adam attended Santa Rosa Junior College, beginning a long line of Victoria soccer player who found their way to the idyllic Northern California junior college. How he chose Santa Rose was not so idyllic. The story, although maybe a tad embellished, goes like this: Adam and friends Scott Longpre and Jeff Mallett (another pair of lifelong friends that soccer delivered to me) were a couple years out of high school. Longpre and Mallett had been playing at UVic and Adam was in Vancouver with the Canadian Olympic program. All three were looking for a change. The story goes that they wrote to lots and lots of schools looking for a chance to play. To their surprise they got quite a few responses.

So how did they decide? Well, these three geniuses decided they would use the most scientific method they could find. They lined up all the packages that they had received and decided they would go to the school that sent the biggest package. Congratulations Santa Rosa Junior College and Coach Craig Butcher.

It actually worked out great for all of them. All had very successful playing careers at Santa Rosa. Longpre is now a coach and teacher in Victoria. Jeff hit it big as an early employee with this company called Yahoo! (maybe you've heard of the Internet giant). Adam is here in Las Vegas.

That decision obviously led to my later, somewhat off-the-cuff move to got to UNLV. It was the first time in my life I made a call without using my usual deliberate rationale. By going to UNLV, I did something impetuous in the way that my brother Adam would do things. Adam constantly did things by impulse. Where I was much more deliberate and maybe conservative, Adam always pushed things a little harder. He never did enough to get in really significant trouble, but if my parents told him to not do something, he inevitably would do it. Like if they told him, "Don't go down to the beach tonight for that party," I'd see him the next morning with his arm all scraped up from having fallen while down at the beach. Classic Adam.

Adam was just Adam growing up and remains that way today. He is warm and inviting. He is well liked and loved by just about everyone who enters his life. For me, getting that time to reconnect with Adam was the highlight of all the truly great things that happened during that time in Las Vegas. It is a connection that we share today and will for the rest of our lives. Without both Adam and I making irrational, impetuous decisions, we would not have gotten that chance.

UNLV and Las Vegas delivered that and so much more to me. Being able to restart my life in the desert of Las Vegas was critical to taking the next steps in my journey.

14

RUNNING DOWN A DREAM

My decision to go to UNLV was really empowering. Not that I needed a boost in confidence or a change of focus. I had plenty of both.

More important, it proved to me that I was on the right track and that my decision-making was good. You could say that my decision to stop taking Prednisone was the same thing, but it was a little different. In a lot of ways, I was fortunate that all of that worked out. My decision to stop taking medication had nothing to do with James Fields dying and I know that.

In contrast, going to Las Vegas proved to me that I was right about my physical conditioning, that I could really play again and do it at a high level. I just needed to find a place that was willing to take me. After two years, I was back on track, chasing my dream of playing professionally. By December 1988, I was done playing soccer at UNLV because my eligibility had run out. I had already played two years at the University of Victoria and the maximum time you get to play in college is four years.

I hadn't graduated yet, but I was done with college soccer at that point. The season had ended and I headed back to Victoria for Christmas. They keep playing club soccer in Las Vegas after the season is over, but the competition isn't very good. That's when I got the idea to go back to England. Nobody in my family was particularly fond of this idea. Actually, they hated it. But I was 23 and I still had the bug to play. I had proven to myself that I could play and that I was good enough. I talked with other folks in Victoria who were close to me including Rob McAdams. The patriarch of the McAdams family and Bette's husband, Rob was an ultra successful real estate developer in Victoria who had been extremely supportive of me and my family. After a conversation with him, he made it clear that life is short and that I should follow my dreams. I told my family: "Tough. I'm going and that's that" and jumped on a plane.

When I look back at that moment, I just know that when I was younger, I wouldn't have done that. I would have said, "OK, I'll do what you want me to do," because I didn't want to be the renegade like Adam. The difference is that by this time, I knew I could handle it. I wasn't afraid to go back because of my heart. Not that my parents were being overprotective. I think they just didn't like that I skipped out on my last semester of college and didn't graduate as early as I could have.

To me, that wasn't a big deal. I knew I could come back and finish. More important, I felt like I had to get away from Las Vegas at that point. There was nothing wrong there. In fact, Vegas was great. That's the point. If I had stayed in Las Vegas and finished out my degree, I probably would have been done with soccer. I would have taken the time off, gotten out of shape and probably moved on with life. From the standpoint of wanting to prove myself in soccer, I needed to keep playing. I had to keep chasing the dream. That's the old expression, if you chase your passion, the money will follow. I wasn't worried about supporting myself. I didn't need much. Again, this was me being more like my brother Adam and doing what I really wanted to do. My problem was that I didn't set up anything this time around, unlike when I had gone there and played for Millwall just out of high school.

Once I got to London and moved in with my uncle Malcolm and aunt Laurette (I could handle the smoke this time around), I had phone numbers of some contacts and hit up one of them. He said they had changed the way they were signing players, so he had no interest. So I wrote a letter and a resume and sent it to Charlton Athletic, which at the time was a first-division team. Charlton played at a high level. I just wanted a place to play. They got back to me the next day after they got my letter and told me to come out and train.

That was good enough for me. I came out every day and practiced with them. I got the feeling they didn't think much of me when I showed up. It was like: "This is just a kid. We'll give him a week's trial and send him home." But I know I turned some heads and showed them I could play a little bit. So they asked me to stay for a month while they took a good look at me and waited for my release from the Canadian Soccer Association. I didn't play at all while I waited, not even as a reserve. As much as it mattered to me, I was just glad to be playing at a high level and feel that I was improving.

I did have to play though. So again, I made another contact. Literally just down the road from Malcolm and Laurette's house was Bromley Football Club. This was what is called in England a non-league club. It is not a part of the top four professional leagues but sits just below as the fifth or sixth best league in the land. The league is tough and in order to play in it you better be able to handle yourself. Not as glamorous as the fancy "big" clubs. No, this club was truly blue collar. I loved it immediately.

While I was still practicing with Charlton, I added practices with Bromley on Tuesday and Thursday nights with games on Saturdays. Sometimes I'd hit two practices a day. Basically, I was training seven or eight times a week, which is a lot in soccer (or any sport, really). In some ways, it was probably good I didn't have anything else going on because I really wanted the work. My goal at the time was to be so fit that when I got back, I would be the best player in the Canadian Soccer League.

Of course, if anyone in England's First Division had offered me anything, I obviously would have stayed, but the realistic goal was to go back to Canada and dominate. I was aiming to play for the Victoria Vistas because I figured that after two years in college and some time in England, people would realize that I was ready to play and they wouldn't have to worry about my heart. That was all that was on my mind. From January to May that year, my time in England was basically an apprenticeship. A lot of that was because while I was at UNLV, Barto didn't push me in terms of fitness. I think he was probably a little bit wary of doing that. He was great for me in so many ways – I don't have any complaints about him – but I'm sure there was still this mental block somewhere in the back of his head that he couldn't push me as hard as he might push someone else.

The first time I ever had anybody who treated me straight up the way I wanted was when I started playing for Bromley. The team captain was this big, tall guy named Paul Edwards. He would just rip me every day, really ride me and it was great because it made me feel like one of the guys. When you play sports, you want to be one of the guys. You want to fit in on the team and be accepted. That's part of the fun. What Edwards did made me feel normal again. He'd come in with a new heart joke every day. A lot of the guys were shocked at first, but that's how I wanted it.

Initially, the guys on the team didn't believe me. The way they found out was that they noticed the protrusion in my chest from the pacemaker and they asked me what the hell it was. I said, "Well, I haven't told the boss yet, but I had a heart transplant." They all laughed at me and didn't believe it. I was like, "OK, whatever, I guess I didn't." I wasn't going to fight them about it. But then I felt like I had to tell the manager of the team. I told him the next day and he said, "Well, you can obviously do the job for us, so it doesn't bother me so long as you're happy to play." It's not like I was trying to hide it, but I wasn't advertising it, either. It's not like you can walk into a locker room and say, "Hi, I'm Simon Keith and I've just had a heart transplant and I want to play for your team." That's not a great business introduction.

Bromley was a great soccer experience. Obviously, the main thing is that I played and I played a lot. It was a hard, physical league, which forced me to learn a lot. It was cold for every game, but the biggest factor was the toughness that everybody played with. There was also a real camaraderie with that team. The guys really got along and the fans were fantastic. There might have been only 2,500 a game, but the fans would sing and chant and get so into it. When you have 2,500 people – screaming idiots, really – showing up to watch you play in freezing weather on frozen ground, it gets you completely pumped up to play.

I started playing up front pretty quickly for Bromley and I was scoring a lot. This other guy and I on the team learned how to work together really quickly. His name was Ronnie Merk. He was from New Zealand, where he had played professionally. We just got along really well. I switched to midfield when we had injuries, but the great thing for me is that whenever we really seemed to need a goal, I was the guy who scored it. This is what it means to be a goal scorer. You measure your own performance by only one criteria: Goals. When they are going in and the team is winning, the game is easy. When the goals dry up, the game can be brutal. For now, I was enjoying the ride.

The only downside with Bromley – and England, in general – was the weather. As usual, I got sick while I was there and it took about three weeks to fight through it. The doctor in England said he thought the problem was mostly dehydration. The problem you have with playing in the cold weather is that you don't really want to drink a lot of water, particularly cold water. So I wasn't getting a lot of fluids and that had a double effect on me because of all the medication I was taking to play. Unlike at UNLV, where it was hot and I was drinking water all the time, I wasn't flushing all the medication through my system as fast. In England, the medication was just sitting in my kidneys. Dehydration continues to be my nemesis today.

By May, my time overseas was up. I decided to head back home in May and follow through on my plan to play for the Victoria Vistas in the Canadian Soccer League. Under my plan, this was my next big step. From my perspective, it was pretty much the only step I could take.

In the early 1980s, the first incarnation of the North American Soccer League (NASL) had folded. It had been in business for about a decade and had done a lot to raise the profile of soccer in North America, particularly in the United States. Most people know that Pele, the Brazilian legend, played for the New York Cosmos in the mid-1970s. That was basically the same thing that David Beckham did more than 30 years later with the Los Angeles Galaxy in Major League Soccer. MLS started in 1996, more than a decade after the NASL first went out of business.

The time from roughly 1984 to 1996 is known among soccer players in the United States and Canada as the "dark decade" for outdoor pro soccer. There weren't any outdoor teams and the game was being taken over by indoor soccer (the Major Indoor Soccer League). For now, just understand that most soccer purists didn't think indoor soccer was anything close to real soccer.

That meant that for guys like me and so many of my friends, you had to play for whatever team or league you could find. When I got done with England and headed home, I knew I was headed for the Vistas of the Canadian League.

I figured I would finally be free of all the crap I dealt with after I first had my surgery because all those people who thought I was going to die would have been proven wrong.

Wrong again.

I got home and ran into the same mindset that had been there two years earlier when I left for UNLV.

I played for two different coaches with the Victoria Vistas. The first one, Brian Hughes, didn't last long, maybe a month. Hughes was someone who I had a long relationship with. I had played with his son John for many years. A soccer nut and respected coach, Brian Hughes was good to me and I played in my best, most natural position, just tucked in behind the forwards. Problem was we were not winning. In fact we were losing. And quite often. The team made the difficult decision to make a coaching change.

Enter Bruce Wilson. He was another guy I had known from soccer circles. Understand that Wilson, who has also coached at the University of Victoria for roughly 20 years, was something of a soccer legend in Canada. He was born and raised in Vancouver and was a literal lifer in the North American Soccer League in the 1970s and early 1980s. As a defender, he played for four teams (Vancouver, Chicago, New York and Toronto) in 299 games, the second most in NASL history before the league folded in 1984. He was a little lucky in that the league got started when he was 23 and he was able to play an entire career.

Beyond that, when Canada made the World Cup in 1986, Wilson was named the captain. He also played in the 1984 Olympics for Canada, was named to the Confederation of North, Central American and Caribbean Association Football (CONCACAF) "Team of the Century" (the only Canadian to be named) and was inducted to the Canadian Soccer Hall of Fame in 2000. In other words, this guy was the real deal.

Except for one problem, at least for me. Wilson was a big fitness nut. Now, I understand part of his point about fitness and that's fine, to an extent. You can't play soccer if you're not fit and, as I said before, my ability to play the game had changed from before my surgery. It wasn't that I wasn't fit. I just wasn't the same type of player who never stopped running. I had to be more selective about how I pushed my body. But Wilson took the fitness thing to an extreme, oftentimes at the expense of creative opportunity, which is essential to soccer.

So I start playing for Wilson and it's obvious to me from the first minute that he's scared to play me. He kept telling me again and again that I wasn't fit. Seriously, I had just gotten done playing a full college season and four months in England and I wasn't fit. My game was about quickness. I was faster over the first three or four steps than anyone I would play.

154

Well, when you get into the tight spaces near the goal, where there are lots of players around, what I used to do worked really well in creating opportunities on offense. Whether it was me getting a shot or somebody else, it was hard for the defense to just sit back when I was out there. But Wilson would only play me half the game, at most. I'd get 45 minutes, even though I felt great. The players on the other team would laugh about it to me. They'd come up to me during the game and say, "Why don't you play more?" I'd just shrug my shoulders.

When I went to talk to him, it got even worse. I told Wilson at one point that I needed to play more than 45 minutes a game, that I wasn't happy. He looked at me and said: "Simon, you're undoubtedly the best player on this team, but I don't think you can do it for me for 90 minutes. I don't think you can run." I looked at him and said, "If that's what you think, there's not much I can do about it except prove you wrong."

The rest of the time I was there, whenever we went on runs, I made sure I was the first in the sprints and I made sure he saw it. It was great motivation for me. I knew he wasn't going to change, but I was still going to make him see that he was wrong about me. It didn't matter.

I was upset at the time. Since my transplant, I had adapted as a player. My soccer brain had grown. What I could do was take over games in the blink of an eye using my pace and brain. The problem from a coaching perspective was that I wasn't able to do all the other grinding work that so many players have to do. Some coaches would sacrifice the defensive work rate for talent in the front third of the game, while others weren't prepared to do that. Wilson chose not to engage in what I could offer.

Prior to my transplant, I took pride in outworking everyone on the field every game. The relentless pursuit was my joy. Following my transplant, I had to change my game. At UNLV, Barto had the creativity and built his team using a system that allowed for my talents. Wilson just didn't. For me, it was a constant battle. I simply would not and could not give in to the notion that I was not fit enough. In truth, I wasn't, but never in a million years was I going to admit it.

15

Hello Cleveland

My introduction to professional indoor soccer was like one of those scenes out of an old black-and-white sports movie. You know those old-time films, like *The Pride of the Yankees* or *Damn Yankees*. You have these over-the-top characters who are talking in rapid-fire fashion while chomping on a cigar, full of confidence and selling you on the idea of greatness and glory.

Man, was Al Miller a different guy.

Miller was the general manager and president and everything else you could imagine for the Cleveland Crunch of the Major Indoor Soccer League. My introduction to Miller was on a field in Wichita, Kansas. As I mentioned before, when I got back from England around May 1989, my intent was to play for the Victoria Vistas of the Canadian Soccer League. I wanted to be the best player in that league. That was my dream. Problem is, you don't always have control over your dreams and I wasn't going to get a chance to play regularly enough to make my dream come true.

As I was getting started with the Vistas, there was a guy on our team from California who, like me, had just finished playing college soccer. He said to me, "I'm going to the senior all-star game in Wichita." I was intrigued and asked what it was and he explained it was all the best players from the United States. He told he didn't have to go because he knew he was going to get drafted by the Los Angeles team in the MISL, but he was going to play anyway. I didn't think too much more about it until I got a call a week later from one of the organizers who said I had been recommended for the game.

Cool. To me, it was another opportunity to make money at the game and get something out of soccer. Making money in soccer is about hustling for what you can find – and that's particularly the case in North America. Anyway, one of my teammates from UNLV, Eddie Anibal, also got invited to the game. It was a week of practices and then the actual Senior Bowl game.

I got to Wichita and had no idea what to expect. Everybody out there seemed to be an All-American, except me and Anibal. I wasn't even thinking about getting drafted or playing in MISL. Our coach for the week was Terry Nicholl from the Wichita Wings of the MISL, and he held a team meeting at the beginning of the week. I sat in the back of the room and listened to all these other guys on the team talking. They were all really cocky and I started to think to myself, "Maybe they really are that good."

Remember, the practices were for indoor soccer, which is a totally different game than playing outdoors. The game is much more about quickness because you're playing in a confined area and the game is much faster because the ball is in played off the boards around the outside. Basically, you're playing on a field the size of a hockey rink (about 70 yards) rather than a full-sized field (about 110 yards). For me, this played right into my strengths. The indoor game is all about quickness in a small space and I was able to adapt to it pretty quickly.

I seemed to be in much better shape than most of these guys. Maybe because I had been playing outdoors. Either way, Anibal and I would go back to our room every night and talk about how shocking some of the players were. One of us would inevitably say: "You see that guy who is a two-time All-American? What a joke." It made us mad because we knew how much more we had done in college than they had. It registered to me that UNLV was an outpost when it came to the college game.

Anyway, we're going through practices. There's a reporter from Sports Illustrated there to do a story on me and some other media around to cover the event. There are so many people there who I have never met that you literally got introduced to somebody new every 10 minutes. It was like, "Hey, I'm Joe Blow, good to meet you."

After one practice, a guy came up to me and said, "I'm so-and-so, tell me about your heart surgery." I was exhausted and, as a result, I kept it short and sweet with my, "One out, one in" answer. Look, I just wanted to go have a shower. The guy asked me a couple of more questions and let me go. He was about 5-foot-8, stocky enough that he barely seemed to have legs. He was smoking cigars, dressed in really expensive clothes that didn't quite fit right and he had all these big rings on his fingers.

The next day, I realized that was Al Miller from the Cleveland Crunch. His team owned the No. 1 pick in the draft. Now, I had no idea what was going on, so I didn't sit there and start thinking, "Oh, I could be the No. 1 pick." Really, I was just playing, trying to do as well as I could and see what might come as a result of this whole deal. Little did I know that Miller had already done some homework on me by calling one of his old friends, UNLV coach Barry Barto.

Barto and Miller knew each other from the mid-1970s when Miller was the coach of the Philadelphia Atoms of the North American Soccer League. Barto was one of Miller's players for three years before Miller left to coach the U.S. national team. Basically, Miller and Barto really understood each other in terms of players and who would do well under their respective coaching styles or, in this case, the way Miller wanted to build a team.

"I'm sure Barry gave me the whole package of information about Simon," Miller said. "What I remember most is when we had that combine with all the top college players, I just kind of fell in love with this kid because he had a great instinct for the game. I really prided myself on knowing if someone had not just the ability to play, but the ability to fit into a team the way you needed to. I saw something about him that was pretty special.

"To me, I was always big on character. All my success in college and pro coaching, anytime I was picking a player, it was all based on really getting to know the player as a person. I did a lot of research on Simon. Sure, he was a great story, but that wasn't going to mean much if I didn't think he could play or be part of the team. I didn't pick him for publicity. I picked him as a player because this was a guy who didn't necessarily want the publicity. He was going to get it because of the fantastic nature of his story, but that's not what he wanted to be known for. He wanted to be known as a player first ... not that it was easy to pick a guy who had a heart transplant. I remember talking to our lawyer and he was saying, 'I'm not sure we can get him insured.' There were some moments before I took him when I said, 'Am I being completely crazy?' You question yourself anytime you're drafting a player. Did you do all your homework, do you really know the kid – all that stuff. This situation was way beyond that. I was about to draft a player with a pacemaker. Not just draft him, but take him with the No. 1 overall pick. Who does that? But that's how good I felt about him as a player and as a person."

So as the day went by when I was in Wichita, people were coming up to me and saying, "Good luck, have a good year in Cleveland." I'm thinking, what the heck are you talking about? When I saw Miller again the next day, he started telling me, "You're going to be the No. 1 pick." All of sudden, I'm thinking this is big deal. I was looking at all the rings on Miller's fingers and thinking this was my big break. Just finding indoor soccer was a big break, because with my quickness, I was completely confident that the indoor game was made for me. The other thing that helped is that because the game was so fast, you had to be thinking offensively all the time. Because I have been watching and playing since I was four years old and because I was coached by my intense English dad, a former player himself, being able to think through situations quickly was natural to me.

Before I go too far down the whole path, realize that soccer purists don't exactly respect indoor soccer. You get people who come over from England who say, "That's not real soccer." They look down at it as a bastardization of the game. Whatever, I was looking for a job. The indoor game really appeals to fans in the United States because it's fast, there's a lot more scoring and the action is constant. It's like NBA or college basketball, how there is always something happening. You usually don't go more than two minutes without some excitement. Same with the NFL, the game is fast, intense, hard-hitting. But if you're from England or some other country where people grow up on soccer (which is most of the world), then you appreciate the artistry of the game. You see the big picture of passing and setting up shots off certain formations. All of that is gone in indoor soccer. Indoor soccer is like that old toy game Rock 'Em Sock 'Em Robots. There's this big flurry of action and then one of the robots gets his head knocked off. In indoor soccer, it's this big flurry of action and then a goal gets scored or the goalie makes a fantastic stop.

The night of the Senior Bowl, as we prepared for the game, I vowed to just have fun and enjoy myself with no expectations. I played exceptionally well. In the third quarter of the game with the score 2-1 for our team, I seemed to take over the game. In a span of eight minutes, I set up two goals and scored one of my own. The goal I scored was a classic indoor move, where I received the ball at the top of the box with a defender right on my ass. A quick turn and shot drilled to the top corner.

My play earned me the Most Valuable Player award. It was July 7, 1989, exactly three years to the day of my heart transplant. After three years, through three different countries, fighting through bureaucracy and health issues and pacemaker issues and all a whole host of other issues, here I stood, the best player in the country. Talk about a moment.

I got drafted No. 1, just like Miller told me. Today, when I watch any professional draft from the MLS to the NHL to the NBA, I get a wry smile on my face. There was a day when I got to walk up to that podium, put the jersey over my head, don the team hat and shake the commissioner's hand. You pretend to be cool, but you're truly in over your head. One thing I was clear about though; I felt I was finally all the way back from the whole ordeal. I had come a long way from that field in England when I couldn't run a 100 yards.

I sat down for lunch with Miller, the owners of the team (George Hoffman and Stuart Lichter) and their wives. Hoffman and Lichter were both securities and development guys around Cleveland and Akron, Ohio. Lichter did a lot of business in California, too. During lunch, they gave me the hard sell. I was the new franchise player. I was this, I was that, I was going to cure the common cold. They were giving me gifts and money. Take this, take that. Shirts for your mom and your brothers, here's $50, go have a nice dinner, here's a bottle of wine … whatever you need.

Miller offered me a contract right then and there. He told me, "No rookie has ever made more than the minimum salary, which is $2,000 a month. We'll give you a $1,000 bonus, maybe, for being number one." I didn't get any of that stuff. I didn't understand contracts, I didn't know about leverage. I was 24 years old and having my first meeting about my contract with Mr. Slick. Like I said, Miller was a beauty, but I didn't sign right then.

Basically, Miller knew how badly I wanted to play. He could read it all over my face and by watching me work out that week. I ended up talking to my dad and he was thinking the same way I was, just go play. When you love the game, you figure if you just go do your thing, the money will follow. In fact, it was my dad who went down to Cleveland to negotiate for me. He goes down there and they promise him all these things like they'll get me $5,000 on a shoe deal and I'll make $20,000 here from sponsorships and endorsements. They'll get me this, they'll get me that. Unfortunately, none of that is actually in the contract, it's just a bunch of promises. While my dad is down there, Miller wines and dines him, they play golf, Miller gives him his word on this and on that. I get signed then showed up later and said, "Where's my $5,000 shoe deal?" the answer was, "Oh, that's not in writing. You can't trust people on stuff like that." This was a valuable lesson for me.

I also learned pretty quick that I had a lot more leverage than Miller was telling me. Other players in the league were coming up to me saying I could have made $50,000 as a rookie. At $2,000 a month, I was going to make about $18,000, and that's what I got, along with a bonus of less than $10,000. One of my teammates, Mike Sweeney, came up to me and said the team had all this stuff planned for the media – The Washington Post, CBS, ABC, NBC, everybody ready to go. If I had just walked out for one day, they probably would have tripled my salary.

"You had them in the palm of your hand," Sweeney told me. "You were drafted No. 1, you had this fantastic story, the press had been good for you, you were a good player. You could have had that." Oh well, what can you do now? I figured I would play well and get the $50,000 the next year.

I made my way back to Victoria after being away from the Vistas for a week. This was not a popular move among my teammates. I understood but I am not sure many players would turn down that kind of opportunity. I took the grief they gave me. I efficiently finished off my season with the Vistas, ending the season tied for the scoring lead on the team. Off I went to Cleveland for more questions and more unwanted publicity.

After I arrived in Cleveland, the first order of business was a physical. This proved to be interesting. I met the team doctor for the first time and I don't think they briefed him on what was going on. In my contract, obviously I had some liability waivers and stuff like that, which was pretty common given my situation. But they really didn't talk to the team doctor about me at all before they drafted me. I'm telling you, Miller had some serious nuts.

Anyway, I go to a meeting with the doctor and he starts to ask me about my heart condition. I started to explain to him, it's not really a "condition." I didn't have some minor problem, I had a transplant. The doctor looked at me and said, "Son, I think you're mistaken about what a transplant is." I said, "No, I think I have a pretty good idea about it." This was the first time I ever had to actually prove to someone that I had a heart transplant, but it was far from the last time.

After I had been exposed to the indoor game, I realized that it was perfect for me. The biggest reason is that the way you substitute in indoor soccer is more like hockey. You are on for two or three minutes, playing as furiously as you can, then you rest for a couple of minutes. Then back on and so forth. In a lot of ways, it's like being a great middle-distance runner, like a 400- or 800-meter runner in the Olympics. You're just all-out for a short period of time instead of having to keep this long pace in the outdoor game. With the restriction I now had in my game because of my heart, this was great.

Our coach was another player, Kai Haaskivi, this big, blond guy from Finland who was about 10 years older than me. He had played for the Finnish national team, came to the United States in the late 1970s to play in the North American Soccer League and then made the transition to the indoor game. He was great to play for because he really understood the game and he understood the mentality of being a player really well because he still was playing. Being a player-coach isn't easy. It's hard enough to pay attention to your job by itself, but now you have to look at the whole team.

The other great thing about Haaskivi is that he didn't really baby me the way some other coaches did. All these years later, I think he actually has a better understanding of it than most people.

"Simon's story is one of those truly unique, less-told stories in the history of human performance and conquest," Haaskivi said. "When you think about the heart and everything that goes into playing, it's amazing what he was able to do. The indoor game is basically doing 30 400-meter dashes at full go for two hours. It's like constantly doing suicides in basketball and football. That's our game in a nutshell.

"Then, on top of that, you're doing it three or four times a week and practicing in between. There would be times we would play three games in four nights. By the third game, you don't even really warm up that much because you're trying to preserve the guys' quads and hamstrings. The body has no chance to recover with that kind of schedule, so you just go out and play and hope that it's close in the third period.

"When I was coaching, I don't think I really understood just how much Simon was dealing with. I didn't really understand it myself, so I relied on him understanding his body and what he could take and he would never say anything to me about it being too much … When you're young and you're playing a sport, you're not focused on the individual story. You're focused on performing and you realize that people don't care if you have slept or eaten or whatever else you're going through when they buy that ticket. When you put the shirt on and go play, you're judged like everybody else. You put the shirt on and the fans expect you to perform. With Simon, they might have known a little bit about his story, but as soon as the game starts, he was just another player to entertain them. To me, that's a testimony to how hard he worked. He didn't want sympathy, he wanted respect as a player."

As we were getting closer to the season, I really thought I was going to be great at this game. And Cleveland seemed perfect for me. The great thing about Cleveland is that they loved indoor soccer. We played at the Richfield Coliseum, which was the same place where the Cavaliers played. Although the Cavs had a good team at the time with Brad Daugherty and Ron Harper, there were a lot of nights when the Crunch outdrew the Cavs.

It had been that way for awhile, even though the Crunch had technically only been around for a year when I got there. What happened is that the Cleveland Force was the indoor team from 1978 to 1987. Miller had actually been the general manager of the team for a couple of years under an owner named Bart Wolstein. The problem was that Wolstein was the kind of guy who interfered a lot and eventually he and Miller butted heads. Miller left to go work in Colorado Springs, Colo., with the U.S. national program. While he was gone for about nine months, Wolstein suddenly shut down the Force in July 1988 because he couldn't get a better agreement with the MISL players association. All of a sudden, a bunch of players called Miller and begged him to come back to Cleveland and bring the team back as the Crunch with new owners.

Miller came back and got it done. They had some business issues to get past, such as assuring the sponsors and the fans that they weren't just going to fold again like the Force had done. Miller worked that out pretty quickly and got the team going. After one season, they drafted me and here I was back in the limelight again.

The attention was exactly what I didn't want for a lot of reasons. First, I was "The Heart Guy" all over again and it was just annoying. Second, it was a distraction from me actually becoming a good player and becoming part of the team. Third, I wasn't the best player on the team and I was a rookie on top of that, so I kept getting the feeling that my teammates resented me. In reality, they probably didn't all that much, but I was self-conscious about it.

Let me break it all down. As for "The Heart Guy" stuff, I've been over that ground again and again. It was the same old, boring questions about whether I was scared or how did it feel and did I think I had really accomplished something. Blah, blah, blah. I had the same answers time after time. Sometimes it was like they never even read the stories from the week before in the previous city.

The second part was more annoying. Basically, I would do interviews all day at least twice a week and when we went on the road, I was always sent out in advance to meet with the media and have them do the story. I was the circus freak that everybody wanted to see. Fine, I went along with the gig, but the problem was that I was rarely with my teammates on days off. Half the time when those guys would go to the bar, I couldn't be there. Or maybe they played golf and I couldn't play because I had to do this or that interview.

Again, that's the camaraderie you talk about having with teammates. You sit around and BS with each other, laugh, tell jokes, rip on each other in a fun way. I know a lot of people who are not professional athletes who just don't understand that point, but it's about team building. It's part of how you learn to trust a guy.

Now, I did have some moments. Basically, I became the "Wingman of Cleveland." I'll let Hector Marinaro Jr. – our best player and one of the greatest players in indoor history – explain. He was a phenomenal scorer and he also happened to be from Canada. He was actually born and raised in Mississauga, Ontario, just on the north side of Lake Ontario. He was only a year older than me, so we had a lot in common. He was the son of a great player (Hector Sr.) from Argentina, so he was raised in the game the same way I was.

Anyway, here's the story from Marinaro: "We'd go out and I'd always used Simon's story once we'd get to talking to girls. I'd start telling them about how he'd had a transplant and how tough he was, and they'd never believe it at first. Then I'd make him open his shirt so they could touch the pacemaker. It literally was like a square box right in the middle of his chest. I just thought that thing was freaking unbelievable. So he'd open his shirt, the girls would feel it. Once a girl saw that, it was this great conversation piece. Simon was great about it. He took it all in stride and he was a great teammate. We enjoyed having him, and we had a lot of good times with him, mostly off the field."

I have no idea how many women I helped Hector break the ice with, but I was happy to play the wingman for my teammate. I took one for the team, so to speak. If that kept Marinaro from getting upset about the other attention I got, OK.

That's because I got way more attention in Cleveland than what I deserved for how I played. As I'll explain in a little while, I got sick, I got hurt and then I got fed up in Cleveland. It didn't end up being a storybook career for me. I'm not complaining about that. What I'm trying to say is that I was in this really uncomfortable position with my teammates, the guys who were actually playing and producing while I was still learning the game. Instead of them getting attention, I got it and I got it for something that had nothing to do with me playing or how good or bad I was at the time.

Not that the attention was always so great. Here's how it would go a lot of the time. We'd get up in Cleveland and do a 10 a.m. practice. Then we'd head to the airport and fly to say Kansas City for a 7 p.m. game that night. We'd head to the hotel for a few hours. The players would generally go relax, sleep for a couple of hours just to get ready for the game.

For me, I'd get to the hotel and there would be cameras waiting there to talk to me and tell my story all over again. It would be the local TV crews, a newspaper, a radio station or two. What am I supposed to say? "Oh, come back tomorrow, I have to go take a nap." Whether I liked it or not, I was there to promote the team, even if that meant promoting me first. I didn't like it, but I went along with it. Whether there was resentment from the other guys or not, I was really self-conscious. Again, Marinaro was great about it.

"I just felt bad for him because everywhere we went, the press was all over him," Marinaro said. "I can't imagine for a young kid just coming into the league to have that kind of pressure. It wasn't like the local paper was covering him. It was all the national media. So everywhere we went, the national media, the local media, everybody wanted a piece of him. I felt bad for him because he really couldn't just sit back and enjoy being a professional player. I think he had a lot of stress. It just seemed like he didn't get the most out of it because of all the press.

"He had a lot of talent, and he definitely deserved to be there. But it just didn't seem that he was having a great time on the field. Off the field, when we got away from everything, we all hung out and we had a good time. But every time we went into practice or on the road, the national media was there. I felt from a league standpoint, it was great. It was great for us because nobody – *60 Minutes* or *Nightline* or whatever show it was – would be coming to an indoor soccer game if it wasn't for him. We were getting national press thanks to him. That never would have happened unless it was for his incredible story. I wasn't jealous of it at all, because it was getting our game out there a lot more due to him. I don't think the players had any animosity towards him. He was well-liked, he was definitely part of the team, and everybody was really quite amazed about his story and what he was able to accomplish basically with somebody else's heart. It's an incredible story. I don't know if anybody else (felt jealous), but nobody ever came to me in that regard. A lot of guys, or at least I did, felt bad for him because I felt like he was under a lot of pressure just because of all the national media that was on him."

All these years later, I appreciate the thoughts from him. Again, I don't know how a lot of the other guys felt, but I know my career didn't go the way I planned. As a result, when I look back at it, the attention I got was way out of proportion. Really, nothing about my experience in Cleveland went the way I planned. From early on, I thought I was really going to make it big in the league. I thought I would score 30 goals, put up a bunch of assists, get 50 points in 52 games and do it year after year. My first game was a perfect example.

We played an exhibition game against San Diego that year. We were at home in the Richfield Coliseum and 19,477 fans showed up. Seriously, for an exhibition game. Miller knew how to promote and the team did some promotion with a bank, which has got to be the only way you could imagine getting that many people to an exhibition indoor soccer match, particularly at the Richfield Coliseum, which was a freaking dump. But man, was the place jumping. It was crazy. The atmosphere was like nothing I had ever seen in soccer personally. Yeah, people get fired up for World Cup matches, but that makes sense. You go to a World Cup match expecting it's going to be nuts. You'd be surprised if it wasn't. But a meaningless game in a sport that nobody in America really loved … and they get that atmosphere? They had the music blaring, the fans were screaming in warm-ups, they turned the lights out for introductions and put a spotlight on us when we were introduced. It was nuts, truly nuts.

And that game provided me with a great highlight to kickoff my career. Late in the game, I took a pass along the left side and one-timed it off my right foot, kissed it off the inside of the goalpost and scored a goal against San Diego Sockers goalie Victor Nogueira. At the time, Nogueira was the premier goalie in indoor soccer and one of the greats of the game, indoor or outdoor.

Trust me when I tell you that scoring a goal against Nogueira in your first game, exhibition or not, was like getting an interception against Tom Brady or hitting a home run off Roger Clemens the first time out. That's a stunning thing and I was pretty damn excited about it. Nogueira, who was from Mozambique, played professional soccer in the United States for 25 years. He was amazingly quick and unbelievably durable. Playing goalie in indoor soccer, which he did for 18 years, is brutal. You're not actually stopping a shot, you're just taking a hit. It's one shot after another with a soccer ball traveling 60 miles per hour at you from six yards away.

That play became a season highlight for the team. They used it again and again on commercials and other promotional stuff and Miller was quoted as saying the play was "sheer magic." It was a little annoying because it got the whole, "The Heart Guy" scores stuff going again, but my confidence in actually playing was still very high. What I remember feeling after that score was that this would be easy. The game was suited for me in terms of quickness and I even liked the more physical side of the game. There was a lot more elbowing and physical play. I was fine with all of that.

There were some tricks to playing indoor soccer, like how to match up with guys on the defensive end, how you would switch from one player to the next. You'd also do stuff that was considered crazy in the outdoor game, like shooting between guys' legs. But that was the subtle part about the game. The essence of it was still soccer, just in an intensified, quick form. It was a sport for smaller, quicker guys and I was all over that.

Well, not so much.

It's not that the game itself was too hard. I think I would have been fine actually playing.

The problem was that, as was typical for me, I got sick. This time I got pneumonia during the season. I was still expected to do all the interviews and the traveling. Plus, like the stubborn (yeah, and stupid) guy I am, I thought I could play through it. I never got the rest I really should have gotten. Between that and a groin injury I got later in the season, I played maybe 25 games in my first season there. I was extremely frustrated with it, but what could I do?

On top of all this, I was head over heels in love with Kelly. While all these things were going on with me in soccer and the press, I had met Kelly back in Victoria. This was the first time I had ever been really serious with a woman. Not because I didn't care before, but because I was never in any place in time that I felt like I could be serious.

Go back over my life from the time I graduated high school. I took off for England, so I obviously couldn't get involved with someone back then. I came back to Victoria and started going to school, but then I got sick pretty soon after. Once I got sick, there was no chance I could have any kind of serious relationship. There were a couple of cute nurses I saw at the beginning, but that wasn't happening. So for the 18 months leading up to my transplant and all those months afterward, I had no chance. Then I headed off to college … you get the picture. I wasn't exactly serious-relationship material. In fact, although I was always very respectful of women, I kind of viewed relationships the way I viewed injuries. Basically, you have one, you go through it, but eventually you shake 'em off.

With Kelly it was different.

16

LOVE AND LOATHING IN ITALY

The unofficial end of my soccer career came in Spring 1990. We were getting toward the end of my first season with the Crunch. I had gone through pneumonia and a groin injury. I hadn't played much, but I was still the talking head they trotted in front of the media whenever they needed somebody to advertise for the team or the sport. Again, I was the dummy who went along with it because I didn't want to be short-sighted and give up the opportunity. I was only 25 at this point and still didn't have a clue. I just figured this was part of playing.

So during a three-day break, when the Crunch handed me a ticket to go to Milan, Italy, I just did what I was told. In this case, I was supposed to go there to help promote the World Cup, which was being played that year in Italy. Just like four years before that when I was in the midst of waiting for a heart transplant, the tournament ran for a month. This time it started in June and ended by early July. In addition, this was a big year for the United States because the U.S. national team had qualified for the World Cup for the first time since 1950. Even though I was Canadian, I was going over there to promote the U.S. team since I was playing soccer in the United States.

Now, most people will hear about me *having* to fly to Italy and sarcastically say, "Oh, cry me a river." I get it, the whole thing sounds really glamorous and fun. Trust me when I say that it was anything but. Not that there was anything wrong with Milan or Italy, generally, but I never saw much of it. Basically, I flew to Italy, taking a day to get there, sat in a hotel for two days waiting to do interviews and then flew back. The great part about it was meeting all these players from other countries, like Brazil and Columbia and wherever else, but it's not like we really even got to hang out. Those guys were going out at night and I was just trying to get used to the time change. By the time I got settled, I was back on a flight. It was totally a business trip.

When I went on television, it was this weird situation where I had headphones on, I was getting asked a question in Italian, the translator would then talk to me, I would answer and then the translator would give my answer. There was no flow, no life to the interview at all. It was just me sitting there in this odd situation. I remember going back to my hotel room, looking out the window and thinking to myself, "Man, this just sucks." There was no way for me to escape being "The Heart Guy" and having everybody look at me like a circus freak. This was going to be the way it was for me at every level if I continued to play. If I got to be more prominent, it would just be the same questions again and again.

The other thing is that I was never going to say no. It wasn't my nature. I knew that as long as I played, instead of having a fight with the media person or the general manager, I was going to continue to do whatever they asked me to do. So the best way to get out of this was going to be to remove myself from the situation.

On top of that, and probably more importantly, I really missed my girlfriend (and now my wife) Kelly Dempers. This was the first time in my life I really cared that much about a woman and I have to say that it was really strange for me to feel like that. I always treated my girlfriends very well, but this was different. I had enjoyed the inevitable "first love" and infatuations we all have, but my past relationships were more surface. Part of the problem wasn't really my fault. By circumstance, I wasn't exactly the greatest boyfriend that any woman could imagine. It wasn't just that I was moving constantly from one place to another, but I never even knew how to say goodbye the right way.

As I said when I was younger, I was too selfish and my ego was too big to see anyone else. My way of breaking up with a girl was to ask her for a ride to the airport for my next soccer journey, get there and say, "Thanks." Then I'd jump on a plane and in many cases, never speak to her again. I wasn't being callous, just maintaining a relationship wasn't a priority at the time. There was this one time when I was at the University of Victoria and the team had just gotten back from a road trip. A bunch of us went out for drinks. When we traveled in college, we wore ties and this was one time that we all went out after we got back, so we were all pretty dressed up.

Well, I ended up having a few drinks, met a girl and went back to her apartment. It was pretty much a typical college hook up and, me being me at the time, I didn't think to call her afterward. About a week later, we were getting ready to go on another road trip and I couldn't find my tie. It was the only one I had, so I called her back finally and asked if I could pick up the tie. She said sure. When I showed up at her place, she wasn't there, but the door was open and she had turned my tie into a noose and hung an inflatable doll from the ceiling with it with a sign with my name on it. I thought it was hilarious. I still didn't call her.

When I was playing college ball at UNLV, I found the girls were way too materialistic. There were lots of girls, but they would always say, "What kind of car do you drive." I would say, "Oh, I rode my bike today" and they'd just say, "See you later." It was so easy to figure them out and it didn't bother me one bit.

On a humorous note, people used to wonder after I had my heart surgery about whether I could have sex again. The answer is a resounding yes. The odd part is that I don't remember the first time I had sex after the transplant. Honestly, I don't. There was one pretty funny story shortly after my surgery. I had been going out with this one girl for awhile and we were at my parents' house. They had gone to a party, some kind of scavenger hunt thing. The rule at my parents' house was that you couldn't have sex there. That was a non-starter. Well, we ended up in bed, rules be damned, and wouldn't you know that my mom came home because she was looking for a bunch of stuff for the scavenger hunt. She opens the door to the bedroom and I say, "Oh, hi mom." She gets that nervous, "Oh, excuse me, oh, oh," then shuts the door and says as she's leaving: "You kids have a nice evening. We'll be out very late."

I think my mother was actually happy about it, even if she was embarrassed as hell. The girl wasn't too happy, but I was laughing inside. The best part is that I didn't get in trouble at all. My brother Adam was so pissed. He said, "I would get killed if that happened to me and here's Simon getting presents for it."

Still, that was all pretty meaningless stuff. In May 1989, everything changed. After I had returned to Victoria and started playing with the Vistas, there was this one night after a game where we had a mixer at a local pub (the Coachman Inn) with some of the sponsors. Kelly was there because her father's company – Ensign Chrysler – was a sponsor of the team. Not that Kelly knew anything about sports. At the time, Kelly wasn't a fan and rarely went to games of any kind. But she had free tickets and had gone to the game with her friend Heather.

Kelly worked at the Ministry of Finance Provincial Treasury at the time. She had a great job with the British Columbia government and one of the guys she worked with was another player on the Vistas named Frank Woods. Frank was an old friend and an awesome player. He played on the Whitecaps even before they were in the NASL and was a highly rated player in the national program. He was a winger, and the fastest player in the first ten yards you ever met. As fate would have it, Kelly and Frank were talking in the pub when I walked up and Frank introduced me to Kelly. Awesome, I was totally smitten with her and, fortunately for me, totally on my game. At least that's what I'm thinking because Kelly stuck around for another hour as I talked, joked and generally entertained her.

I had so much game going that I didn't get her number and when Frank told her I was hoping she would show up for the next game, she looked at Frank and said, "Who?" Frank tried to talk me up by saying, "You remember, the guy who was the best player on our team, who you ended up talking to after the game?" She just said, "Simon who?"

As she likes to tell people to this day, "I didn't remember what he looked like or what his number was."

Yep, I had some work to do. On top of that, her friend Heather almost killed everything before it even got started. Heather kept telling Kelly, "Don't date a soccer player, they're the worst, all they do is sleep around and cheat on you." Heather is just killing me for being a soccer player even though she doesn't know me. Fortunately for me, Kelly's best friend at the time, Roslyn Peleshaty, assured Kelly that I was a "good" guy. Ros had known our family for many, many years and knew the type of person I was. Thankfully Kelly listened to Ros on this one.

Anyway, here's the deal with Kelly: She's completely self-confident, her own woman who doesn't take any nonsense from anybody and who knows she would do just fine in the world on her own. She's beautiful, too, but the strength of her personality jumps off the page when you talk to her. She is completely comfortable with who she is. I hadn't met many women like that up to then, certainly not any women who I found as attractive as her on every level.

So Kelly showed up at the next game, said she still didn't remember who I was until I found her at the bar and we started talking again. We stood on the deck of the Coachman Inn for a couple of hours. My luck couldn't have been any better. It was a beautiful night and I was making her laugh, telling jokes and singing. We had a great time. Kelly didn't drink much because she had to drive, but she didn't need it. We just had an awesome time.

As the end of the night was coming and she was about to head home, I asked her for her number. She gave it to me and I sort of fumbled as I said that I would call her sometime. I guess I sounded kind of arrogant and she jumped right on that and said, "Don't strain yourself." Like I said, she's completely self-confident. It's one of the things I still love most about her.

I called her a couple of days later and asked her if we could go to a movie. She agreed and I was all set to meet her at her parents' house. I was supposed to pick her up at 7 o'clock. I'm excited, looking forward to it and then, as I'm getting ready, I got a call to do an interview with the *New York Times* of all organizations. As usual, dumb-ass me wouldn't say no to the interview, certainly not the *Times,* and I went through with it.

Meanwhile, Kelly is waiting and waiting, getting more and more pissed. She was about to give up when I finally called her at 8. I tried to explain it to her, but she said, "Who do you think you are, telling me you were talking to the *New York Times*? What would they want to talk to you about?"

Now, you have to realize two things. Number one, this was maybe the first person in Victoria I had gotten to know who had no idea who I was. Number two, that fact was awesome. It was everything I could do to beg her to wait for me. I just asked if we could go walking on the beach or do something else.

Meanwhile, on the other end, Kelly's mom, Sue, heard how she was talking to me and told Kelly, "Why are you being such a bitch? How do you know he's lying?" That might be the greatest assist I've ever gotten. That got

Kelly to back down enough that she actually agreed to go walk on the beach with me. Of course, as I showed up, she just walked out and slammed the door and started walking. It's like the old saying, anything good in life is worth working for and she was going to make me work at it.

We started walking on Parker Beach. She said, "OK, seriously, who would want to interview you? What's the big deal?"

This was perfect. She had no idea who I was. Kelly had lived in Victoria for 10 years and never paid attention to my story. This was someone with no preconceptions about me or what I was like. She didn't think of me as a piece of china or as someone with limitations. I told her the whole story, but I kept it to my usually "One out, one in" way of speaking and she seemed to go right along with that. I think the key is that Kelly never saw me as sick or frail. She saw me as healthy and fun-loving, as an athlete who really enjoyed life and had a passion for it.

"Simon was casual and flippant about having a heart problem, like it was something he just had to deal with," Kelly said. "As he talked about it, it all started to make a little more sense about why the newspapers would be interested in him, but he didn't make a big deal out of his condition. He wasn't wallowing in it. He was normal about it."

By June, we were dating more seriously and then I went to the college all-star game in July. That was part of a pretty long road trip because after the all-star game and getting drafted by Cleveland, I had to go on a road trip with the Vistas to the eastern part of Canada for a couple of weeks. This was part of Kelly's early introduction to the life of an athlete.

Or, better yet, my introduction to how unimportant some of my life really was to the rest of the world. This one night, the Vistas were playing Vancouver and Kelly watched the game on television. She still didn't know exactly who I was or even what number I wore. She said the only way she could pick me out was by my legs because she thought I had nice legs. Anyway, I scored a goal, but we lost the game. Afterward, I called her and I was in a bad mood because we lost.

That's part of the whole athlete-competition equation she didn't quite get. She asked me at one point, "Why are you so grumpy?" I said, rhetorically: "What two things do I hate most? Losing and talking about losing." I'm expecting she's going to completely understand that. Instead, she said, "OK, so don't talk to me," and hung up the phone. I was being rude and she wasn't going to deal with it. That's another one of the things I love about her. She helps me put this stuff in perspective. Up to that point, I was so obsessed with soccer and competing that I thought the whole world saw this stuff the same way I did. Not so much.

It was kind of the same thing after I got drafted. When I called her and told her, she said, "Why can't you go somewhere nice?" I had to explain to her that it didn't really work that way. You get drafted to play for a team and you pretty much have to go play for that team if you want to play at all. All this stuff that I thought was so basic was foreign to her.

The important thing is that I don't think it really bothered her. Again, she was her own woman, capable of handling her life the way she wanted. It was like when she started coming to Vistas games and she'd see the other women who hung out at the games. It would be a Sunday afternoon and you'd have women coming to games dressed up in high heels and revealing outfits. Seriously, even for a relatively small soccer team in a struggling league, you had groupies. Where some women would maybe get jealous of that, Kelly would roll her eyes and just chuckle about it. She wasn't at all caught up in the mystique of the athlete life.

Part of it is that she grew up in a relatively well-off family, but that's an oversimplification. Her dad had plenty of money, but it was way beyond that. I think she would have been like that if she grew up with nothing. I really got the feeling that if we had broken up at some point, she would have moved on without a hitch. That's how much she had her stuff together. At the same time, she has been an incredibly devoted wife and partner.

It was like when I came back and told her I was moving to Cleveland in the fall. Here I am trying to let her down easy, talking about how I didn't want to hurt her, I wanted to do right by her, all this cliché stuff. She looked at me and said, "I thought we were just having fun." Her confidence was off the charts and it was intoxicating for me.

After I got to Cleveland, Kelly visited a couple of times and she was hilarious. Each of the Crunch players had a person who was their "booster," a woman who helped the guys out and would keep scrapbooks of articles for them and all this. It was really intended to be pretty innocent, but it's the kind of situation that could get a little weird. My booster was a woman named Pate (pronounced like "Patty" but she had to give herself some style).

Anyway, Pate was pleasant enough, but not really my type. She was a little on the heavy side and was obviously looking for more of a connection than I was interested in. Truth is, she wasn't very confident. There was this one time she came up to me at a bar and started crying about how, "You could never be with me because I'm so big." What are you supposed to say when someone is like that? You don't want to hurt somebody, but you don't want to lead them on, either.

Kelly came to visit one time and all of a sudden, Pate was ready to rumble. Not literally rumble, but she was going to stake her claim to me as she saw Kelly as a threat. I'll let Kelly take it from there.

"This enormous woman came up to me and said, 'I'm Pate. I'm Simon's booster,'" Kelly said. "She kept going with, 'You must be Kelly. Simon has talked about you.' Pate was trying to talk down to me and said, 'You know, I helped pick out the furniture for Simon and his roommate, did you notice?'"

"I said, 'No, I walked straight through to the bedroom.'"

Like I said, Kelly doesn't take crap from anyone. She was my soul mate.

As the months wore on, my brain was all over the place. I got sick and wasn't playing very well. I thought one time that I needed to put distance between me and Kelly so that I could concentrate on soccer, so I called her and said, "I have to stop talking to you all the time because I have to focus." Again, all she said was, "OK, do what you need to do." I lasted a week. I thought about her every day. I'd never been like this with a woman, ever.

That just accentuated the problems with having a long-distance relationship. Your mind plays tricks on you when you're that in love with someone. I realized just how deep I was in with her during those couple of days in Milan. I was wasting time on something that didn't mean anything in my life. Soccer was important, but flying seven hours or whatever I did to spend two days in a hotel for some stupid interview about an event I wasn't even playing in wasn't important. That was just a waste of my life and I didn't go through all of that pain and suffering when I was waiting for a heart transplant to waste my time on something so meaningless. I had somebody I wanted to be with. I had a life I wanted to build. That was way more important.

After the season in Cleveland, Al Miller suggested that I go back to Victoria to "recuperate" from the long winter season in Cleveland. I couldn't book my flight fast enough. I got back to Victoria and Kelly and I got more serious. I asked the Vistas if they would trade me. I just didn't think the system in Victoria was going to work for me. "The Heart Guy" stuff was getting to me again and I just wanted to play free from the attention that inevitably surrounded me. So Victoria was good enough to trade me to the Winnipeg Fury and I convinced Kelly to quit her job and move there with me. That was no small sacrifice on her part. First, she was leaving a great job. Second, she was leaving her mom and dad. Third, she was moving from Victoria to Winnipeg, which is 1,500 miles away.

And that only begins to explain the difference. Winnipeg is in the province of Manitoba and sits at the eastern end of the Great Prairie. It's about 100 miles north of the border with the United States and is directly above where Minnesota and North Dakota meet. It sits at the confluence of the Red and Assiniboine Rivers, but that's about it in terms of any natural beauty. It's a pretty humble oasis in the middle of an almost completely flat, desolate part of the world. The closest comparison to Winnipeg in the United States would probably be Indianapolis. Not an awful place, but not exactly a place you dream about ending up. When you compare it to Victoria, which is this stunningly beautiful place, Winnipeg just doesn't compare.

A few days before leaving, I had nose surgery. I had broken my nose in an indoor game in Cleveland and waited until the end of the season to have it fixed. So when I got to Victoria, I scheduled the surgery. The Doctor left the splints in and told me to have the trainer in Winnipeg remove them when I got there. So off we go with a little U-Haul behind us on our new adventure. But as we make our way through the Rockies, we have this terrible smell in the car. It is just awful. We spend the better part of two days trying to figure it out, but no luck. Every time we are in the car it just stinks. Once we arrive and move into the house, I notice the smell is now in the house. So it must be the clothes, or blankets, or something. But still no luck and it's getting worse.

Day Two in Winnipeg and the smell is just awful. Now it seems to be everywhere. All of my clothes, all the sheets. Kelly has washed everything but it all still stinks. But it doesn't matter for the time being. I have to go to take my physical. I meet the team doctors and trainers for the physical. As usual, the physical is always hilarious when I start to explain the transplant.

But this exam gave me problems unrelated to the ticker. I tell the doctor and the trainer that I have splints in my nose and that they will need to take them out. The trainer takes one look up my nose and says, "You have gauze up here and it is green. It looks infected". He took some long tweezers and removed the ugliest, smelliest gauze you could imagine. Suddenly nothing smelled anymore. What an idiot I was and poor Kelly was still at the house busy washing everything we owned because I was so clueless.

That wasn't the end of it. Now they had to take the splints out. Nose splints are impossibly long. They go from the tip of your nose all the way to the top of your sinuses. At that moment, the doctor had to take a phone call, so the trainer said he would take them out. I spent the next 30 minutes laying on the training table in absolute agony as this trainer pulls and pulls to get the splints out. I think at one point he literally had his foot on my head to get more leverage. It is at this point that the doctor walks in from his 30-minute phone call.

The doctor said casually to the trainer, "Did you cut the stitch that keeps the splints secure?" What the freak? I am now ready to kill the trainer. The doctor walks over, and with a little snip in the nose the splints come out as easy as pie. No more nose splints and trainers for me.

Once we got settled in Winnipeg, training began and, once again, more reporters. I guess it just wasn't ever going to be in the cards for me to escape the attention. On top of that, my first game for Winnipeg was against Victoria. I would be lining up against my former teammates. Now, I don't care what anyone says, any athlete that says "it is just another game" when playing against their former team is full of it. There is extra incentive to play well and this was no different for me. On top of this, I was going to face, for the first time in my life, Ian Bridge. Bridge was six years older than me. When I was a kid, like 11 or 12 years old and he was 17 or 18, that seemed like a whole lifetime of difference.

Bridge had as good a career for a Canadian that anyone I had personally known. He had grown up in Victoria and, like me, left for England immediately out of high school. My father had been instrumental in assisting

Bridge, and Bridge had even spent the year living with my Uncle Malcolm while training with West Ham in the English League. Later he was one of the rare players from Victoria to make it to the North American Soccer League, playing for the Seattle Sounders during the heyday of the NASL. His career was long and distinguished. He was the first person I knew personally who in my mind had "made it." I even patterned my career after his.

So as I lined up with my new teammates, playing against my former team with my idol playing center back, the script was set. Funny thing though, after all these years I have no idea what the score was. I do remember that Bridge turned out to be one of the toughest, meanest players I had ever played against. He kicked me all over the park that day. He didn't care that I was damaged goods. Or that we were good family friends. He was professional, efficient and, frankly, one of the few guys I would be happy to never play against again in my career.

That day, my choice for an idol was cemented. And I learned another lesson on how to be a professional.

Later that week, we were scheduled to play the second game of our season. I had picked up a few nicks and bruises during the Victoria game thanks to Mr. Bridge. Nothing out of the ordinary. Or so I thought. My right ankle was bothering a bit more than usual, so the team sent me for a precautionary X-ray. The results came back that I had multiple bone chips floating in my right ankle. It was explained to me by the doctors that because of the heavy doses of prednisone I had taken over the years, my bones were more susceptible to this type of injury. I tried to explain that I thought Bridge was much worse than bone degeneration, but they didn't buy it.

The season continued as all seasons do: Game by game, practice by practice. I was really limping through it, but I kept playing as best as I could. And then I got a visit from the new head coach: A guy by the name of Kenny Wharton.

Wharton's first task was to tell me I got traded. The first rumor was that I was going to get traded to Hamilton. Then it was Vancouver. Then Calgary. Then on July 29, Kelly's birthday, Wharton told me that I was going to be traded to Montreal.

I told the people in Montreal I was injured, but they didn't care. By that time, I had three bone chips floating around in my foot. On top of that, the coach from Montreal, a guy named Roy Wiggemansen, called me and told he needed me the next day. Seriously, he wanted me to just pack up and be there. I had my family to pack up and move, Kelly and I didn't know anybody in Winnipeg who could really help us. I was ticked off the rest of the day with this guy and here it is Kelly's first birthday with us as a couple on our own.

I was so flustered and pissed that we ended up going to McDonald's for dinner. Seriously. Then, we're walking around that night and I turned to her and popped the question in another memorable moment that Kelly doesn't let me forget.

"He turned to me and said, 'You know, it has been a really shitty day. I don't know if things are going to get better. We might as well get married,'" Kelly said. "Then he tried to tell me how he was going to buy me a ring, but he didn't know what kind of ring I wanted. Then he was going to give me an empty box for the ring and give me that over dinner. I was like, 'Who gave you that idea? That's a horrible idea.' At least he called my dad afterward and asked him. He did that nicely."

Hey, she still married me. I had to be doing something right.

"He made me laugh, all the time. He still does. More than 20 years later, I'm still laughing … I never had a hesitation about marrying him. Yes, it's a huge risk to marry someone who has had a heart transplant. Who do you talk to about something like that? But it was easy for me because I knew he was healthier than 95 percent of the people out there. To me, it didn't matter if I had five months or five years. I would rather have five months of being truly happy than wait three or four years to maybe find somebody else," Kelly said.

Kelly and I figured out the Montreal situation. We both loved Montreal. It is simply a beautiful city where, to this day, we have so many great memories. Maybe the biggest highlight for us is that Montreal is where we bought Kelly's wedding dress. As a professional soccer player, that might be an indication that the career is not going quite the way you expected.

Montreal was pretty much like my time in Victoria. I would play 90 minutes one game, five the next and 45 the next after that. It was chaos. It was becoming apparent to me that I was becoming someone that I didn't want to be. I was becoming unhappy with the game. I was becoming inconsistent as a player and, most of all, I was not enjoying it.

The beauty of the whole thing is that I didn't really care by that point. On Nov. 24, 1990, Kelly and I got married. We actually thought about getting married during the summer when we were in Montreal, but my mom wanted to have a big wedding in Victoria. As was typical, our ideas of romance weren't quite in sync. For a honeymoon, I arranged for us to go to a rustic cabin in the wilderness. It was a little too rustic for Kelly, who believes that camping is any hotel that doesn't have room service.

By the early part of 1991, less than a year removed from my jaunt to Italy, I knew that my time as a soccer player had come to a close and we headed for Las Vegas, where I went back to college to finish my degree. It was the end of a great challenge and the beginning of the greatest success of my life.

17

The Power of Stupid

Leaving soccer didn't mean that I removed myself from competition. Actually, I went from the frying pan of professional soccer into the burning heat of Las Vegas' entertainment business. The transition wasn't immediate. My first move was to re-enroll at the University of Nevada-Las Vegas and finish my degree. The good thing for Kelly and me was that my brother Adam and his wife Jill were down there, so we lived with them for the first six months.

I graduated in a year and then started working in the UNLV athletic department. I was working in the fundraising and business development department and that led me to a change in direction. For most of my life, I thought I would teach and coach like my father. Now that I was married to Kelly and got to know people in the business community, my focus shifted. I do remember that my first job at UNLV paid me $28,000 a year, which was shockingly huge for us at the time.

Times eventually changed as I got more and more ideas about what to do. One of the most important people I met along the way was Sheila Strike-Smith. She was the assistant athletic director for UNLV and she hired me as a favor to Adam. She was a Canadian who had played on the 1976 national women's basketball team in the Olympics. She had been the coach of the UNLV women's team for seven years. Later, she married Gene Smith, who is now the visionary athletic director at Ohio State and one of the most respected men in College Athletics. Sheila was wickedly smart. Just a brilliant, brilliant lady who took me under her wing. She taught me how to be a leader, how to actually work, how to interact with people, how to make the transition from "jock" to business professional. Maybe the most important thing she taught me was about goal-setting and then setting up a plan to follow through on that goal. Successful people almost always have a mentor, someone who they look up to and learn from. For me, Aunt Sheila, as my kids refer to her as, was and remains that person.

She really understood my mindset and was able to help me translate my athletic skills and knowledge into business. It sounds like such a simple concept, but when I sit down and write out my goals each year and now each quarter, it seems to help me relentlessly focus on attaining them. It can be a number I want to see in the bank or it can be getting from 183 to 179 pounds or reducing my body fat from 11 percent to 9 percent. I know it seems very simplistic, but it works for me. It appeals to my mindset where you're planning for competition or looking ahead to a whole season. It's about doing the prep work, such as the training. It was a core value she instilled in me that still drives me to this day.

The other part of the transition that was important to me was getting away from all the things that held me back when I was playing. I didn't have the media attention that interfered with playing or made me self-conscious about my place on the team. I was about to embark on a new career and I wanted to do it my way.

To compete.

The business I got into was providing souvenir merchandise for a lot of the casinos and hotels in Las Vegas. I worked for this guy I met through UNLV and learned the ropes. It may seem goofy to provide t-shirts, dice, jackets, all the tchotchkes that the hotels and casinos either sell in the gift shop or give away to people who visit. Literally, you're talking about 100,000 different items that you might order in a year, from ball caps to crystal vases. Anything that can possibly have a casino or hotel logo on it is something you're looking to sell. I became the supplier of crap, but you can make a lot of money being the supplier of crap.

What I also learned in the process is that I wanted to be the guy in charge of that operation, particularly after I felt that I got screwed out of an $85,000 bonus at one point. Kelly remembers me coming home from that and being so angry. I swore that day that I wasn't going to let somebody else determine my future.

This was about the time that I also came up with my concept that I like to call, "The Power of Stupid." When I saw the guy I was working for driving a really nice car and playing golf every day, I didn't sit there and say – I don't know how he does it? – I just went out and did it because I didn't think there was any reason I couldn't. I remember when I left his company, there was a big stink. He and his family wanted to know who I had borrowed money from to start my business. It got really cutthroat. I didn't care. I had my idea about how to do it and I executed my plan.

I figured out every angle I could imagine. I provided things that added value for clients that other competitors just weren't thinking about. Or I would make agreements with hotels to not just handle the gift shops, but all of the events they ran. I got involved with NASCAR, the NBA, the Pro Bull Riders, UNLV basketball, drag races, hockey events, everybody and anybody who was working in Vegas and even some other cities. Again, this may not sound like the most complex business from a distance, but it requires a lot of planning and a lot of patience. It's basically an all-cash business. When you go to China or some of these other countries where they are mass-producing different items, there's no line of credit. You're putting out the cash first and then waiting 60 to 90 days to then turn around sell everything you have. I spent many trips in rural China visiting factories and making cash deals for products I knew my clients back home would need.

You're also watching people like crazy. Anybody who works for you, you have to be careful about security. If you're running the souvenir stands for a major concert or a fight, you have to be on top of the process all the time. Basically, take the stress of playing in a soccer match and multiply it by 100. Sure, it might not be pushing your body as hard in any one moment, but it was tireless work. This was a straight hustle business. There were times I would be gone for 30 straight hours. At the end of that, I might walk into the house with a box full of cash because the armored car had already left while we were counting the money. I remember the first time I came home with about $300,000 in cash and it just freaked Kelly out. I put it in the safe at the house until I could take it to the bank in the morning, but she was just a mess thinking about what bad things could happen.

Me, I just relied on the Power of Stupid.

"Simon never worries about that stuff, like getting robbed," Kelly said. "He would look at me and say, 'What's the worst thing that could happen? You give them the money.'" Then again, she sort of learned the value of my theory of The Power of Stupid.

Or as she likes to say, "When you have an instructor as gifted as Simon, it's not very hard to learn."

Literally, we were handling at least $1 million in cash every week. But you were existing on such a narrow margin sometimes that you couldn't afford to lose $10,000. That could kill you in a week. The other side of it was that you were dealing with the management people from some of these artists and they would want a share of the money, especially in a cash business. What all of this meant is that we were able to move into a wonderful home that was built by our friends Frank Kocvara and his son Frank Jr. in 2000. Since then we have moved one more time again with the Kocvaras whom we have now lived across the street from for almost 20 years.

The more important challenge was raising a family. When it came to that, the Power of Stupid didn't apply. Kelly and I did a lot of research about having children. Ever since I had my transplant, I have dealt with a regimen of four or five medications every day. Today, the drugs include a combination of prednisone (five milligrams a day), allopurinol (100 mg), cyclosporine (150 mg) and CellCept (500 mg).

What you have to understand about that is that those drugs are slowly killing my body. Or at least parts of it. I know someday that I'm going to have kidney failure. That just goes with the territory. It doesn't matter how fit I am or that I've outlived most transplant patients by 15 years – I don't have a magical way of avoiding that. But I'm also not really worried about it. When you think about it, what's the choice? I've had this glorious life with all sorts of accomplishments and I'm going to complain about some of the tradeoffs? Please.

The thing Kelly and I wanted to be aware of is whether any of those drugs could hurt our children. We did every bit of research we could and talked to doctors before we ever tried. Beyond that, there was some small doubt about me because I had gone through chemotherapy for my heart before I had my transplant. The doctors said it could have left me impotent. Fortunately, that wasn't the case.

I remember the first time Kelly got pregnant and we went for the ultrasound. When I found out it was a girl and she was healthy, I broke down in tears. I was standing there holding Kelly's hand and it was just this overwhelming moment. I know plenty of men who completely understand that general feeling, but it was one of those moments that I was really close to thinking I would never have.

Our last child was our son Sean and he was not exactly expected. He wasn't an accident, don't get me wrong. In the early part of 1995, Kelly was pregnant again and she was about four months along. Unfortunately, she had a miscarriage. If there can be a funny part to this, we happened to be at St. Rose Hospital, and our doctor was a very conservative gentleman. When he told us, I said, "Shit happens." I didn't mean to be flippant about it, this was just my way of dealing with it. Kelly looked at me like I was insane and me dropping a swear word in front of this nice, conservative doctor didn't exactly go over well.

Anyway, about seven months later, Kelly started to feel sick. She thought it was some kind of virus or cold. Her plan was to get her tubes tied at that point because we figured we were out of the baby business. When she went in for a checkup and to inquire about the surgery, she found out she was pregnant. We went back for a sonogram, found out it was a boy and this time I was speechless, but obviously happy.

"He hasn't stopped smiling for 16 years," Kelly said.

Sean added a dimension to our life that I was much more comfortable with. Prior to this, it was all girls, all the time. Growing up in a sports-centric, all-boys household the way I did, the girl thing was foreign to me. Kelly and my daughters will readily explain that raising girls was all very new to me and, at times, I was totally out of my element. In fact, there was a classic story about Sam from when she played youth soccer. It was a cold night in Las Vegas and she was out there playing. She came out of the game and went to sit on Kelly's lap and Kelly wrapped her up in a blanket.

A little later, the coach came over and said, "OK Sam, it's time to go back in." Sam looked at him and said, "No, I'm not playing." The coach tried to cajole her onto the field. Sam would have none of it.

"No, I'm cold and I'm not playing and you can't make me," she said. That was the end of Sam's soccer career – and a glimpse into her personality - and I just had to roll with it.

With Sean, now I had someone I understood.

Our three kids are all very different. We have been blessed with three genuinely nice, good-looking (thanks to Kelly) and smart kids. It is amazing how three children, all brought up the same way by the same parents in the same environment, can be so different. Sarah is very glamorous, very loyal and very family-oriented. Sam is a tom-boy with my "direct" personality. Sean has an old man's soul inside a young man's body – a true gentlemen. Kelly and I are intensely proud of each one of them.

They say that "good men raise good men." I believe that is true of parenting. Both Kelly's and my parents did fantastic jobs raising their children.

Ed and Sue Dempers had a very similar story to my parents. Ed and his brothers were orphaned at a very young age while growing up in Rhodesia/Zimbabwe. Sue was raised in South Africa as an only child. After meeting in London, they got married and made a move first to Toronto and later Victoria in the late 1960s. Sue looked after the home and two kids (Kelly and younger sister Michelle) while Ed worked for and eventually became part-owner of a car dealership. They raised their children with the same core values as my parents, and much of the same pioneer type spirit that was a part of me.

I would never change my upbringing for anything and thank the day that my parents had the guts to get on that ship back in 1967. The only significant difference that I use in parenting compared to my parents' generation, and it is more a cultural change than anything, is that I'm very sensitive about giving my kids a lot hugs and kisses. I just appreciate that contact and I want them to feel it all the time, that sense of approval and unconditional love.

Not everything can be perfect, of course. When Sean was a freshman at Bishop Gorman High in Las Vegas, he made the varsity soccer team. As the team was getting ready for the playoffs, however, Sean had a problem. He had a failing grade on the progress report for his algebra class. As a result, he couldn't play. When he got home, I could see he was hurting and embarrassed. He came up to me and just broke down in tears. I could tell how hurt he was and I'm sure he was waiting for me to rip him pretty good. I did just the opposite. I hugged him and said, "I can't say anything to make you feel worse about this, but promise me you will never let this happen again."

More than anything, this is the life I wanted to have. I wanted to be a guy who got married and had a family life. Again, I didn't want to think in terms of limits. Even all these years removed from playing, I push myself. Over the years, I have tried to maintain my physical condition. That was hard when I was running my own business and it was so demanding. About a decade ago, I wasn't necessarily in bad shape, but I was nowhere close to what I had been at my peak. That's when I started to train again. Over the years, I improved my training and now have a personal trainer, Amanda Richardson, who works with me and my son, Sean.

I'll let Richardson give you the rundown.

"I had no idea until I first sat down with Simon and he told me that he had a heart transplant," she said. "I've worked with a lot of clients with different types of medical issues. He is the first of that sort. I'm not scared to work with people who are challenged. I think he likes that because other people were kind of scared to take the chance and work with him. They were afraid that something might happen. We've been working together ever since.

"I think it became more comfortable because I would treat him like a normal person, like anybody else. I think that's what he really needed. He needed someone to really push him and put him through a normal workout. I've trained professional athletes before and I can see that he can do anything. I can push him harder than any of my other clients, hands down. He basically is like training any other athlete. Anything that I have him do, he at least tries and pushes himself. If he can't do it, he trains himself until he can do it. So it's weird because it's like he has no limitations."

There are, of course, medical realities I have to live with. Whether it has been daily medication or more checkups than the usual guy or a series of maintenance surgeries, that's the small stuff. You don't sweat that kind of stuff. Kelly has become an amazing watchdog over my care as well.

We've had some emergencies along the way. There was one year I had to get my pacemaker replaced and I ended up getting an infection. The problem with infections for someone who takes immunosuppressant drugs is that you don't usually feel anything until it is extremely painful. When this happened, I actually had to call Kelly to come home because I was shaking like crazy and sweat was pouring off me. She got me an ambulance, but that was only the beginning.

Another issue you have when you're a transplant patient, particularly a heart transplant patient, is that hospitals and doctors aren't exactly jumping up and down with excitement to deal with you. If the hospital doesn't have someone experienced in transplants, it is very tough. We got to the hospital, and the doctors didn't know what to do. Kelly had to call Dr. Hakim, the man who did my surgery and get him to give her directives.

Here was my wife trying to get the doctors there to talk to Dr. Hakim and they wouldn't do it. Finally, she had to start yelling at them to give me the right medication. Seriously, it was a frantic moment, but it's why she has become so diligent over the years in dealing with my needs. Taking care of me alone is a full-time job. That's not an overstatement, that's truly how it is. As I have become the businessman, Kelly took care of our home. Yeah, she had some jobs along the way, but she still made it extremely easy for me.

So easy that I kind of get lost when she's not around. I think I've broken every appliance in our house, including one time when I nearly blew up the dryer because I had no idea how to use it. I think I've vacuumed maybe a dozen times in all our years together.

"I want home to be as stress-free as it can be for Simon, for it to be his oasis," Kelly said. And she does it. Our partnership has been an amazing life. She has put up with a lot from me, learning to deal with my competitiveness, which should not be understated. I tend to be driven by people who say something can't be done by embracing a moment that seems impossible.

Generally, those moments drive me to be my best. That happened throughout soccer. Like so many athletes, getting negative reinforcement drove me. At the same time, some guys like to look for the negative in a situation to create that drive. I couldn't ever manufacture that in my head. I'm too positive and driven to do that. But if you say that to me, I eat it up. Tell me I can't do something and I'll show you I can.

To me, I took a clinical approach to obstacles. If I could find a way to solve it, I solved it. The foundation for that came from my father, and it was hardened by what I dealt with before and after the heart transplant. I wasn't going to lose focus on what I needed to do.

In some regards, I think that's what has thrown Kelly for a loop as I approached doing this book and, more specifically, reuniting with James Fields' family. I couldn't really explain to her why I was doing this and I think she didn't really want to know for fear that there was some big reason, like I suddenly didn't think I was going to live much longer or that I actually knew I wasn't going to live much longer. She didn't want to hear that if that was the case.

It's not. Really, what this was about was reconnecting after 25 years of being disconnected. I spent 25 years denying that anything was different about me because I never wanted to be perceived that way. I wanted to be a great soccer player, not a just a great story about a soccer player who had a transplant. That required a certain amount of denial about the difficulty of what I went through and a certain amount of denial about how people perceived me.

What it didn't leave room for was introspection. That has never been my strong suit. Again, it's my concept of the Power of Stupid. What you don't know – or at least what you refuse to acknowledge – can't stop you from accomplishing your goal.

At the same time, my life, my goals, my family are completely dependent on the largesse of a wonderful family in Wales that was gracious enough to give me a second chance as they dealt with grief. As a result, I have had the most wonderful life I could imagine. A life I can be proud of.

A life I hope they can be proud of, too.

18

REUNITING WITH THE FIELDS

So here I stand at the final resting place of James Fields.

To my left, Robert weeps quietly over the loss of the unfulfilled future of his 17-year-old son James who passed 25 years ago, on that fateful day, on that fateful field.

As this dignified man sheds a silent tear, still feeling the loss, I am uncomfortably thankful.

How do you say thank you to someone who gave you ... everything?

I wanted Robert Fields to be proud of me. I wanted to make good on the gift I had received. I wanted him to know the gift was not in vain.

I'm not sure that makes sense to a lot of people, mainly because I couldn't quite get my brain around the emotion myself. But that's what I just kept coming back to again and again. As I stood in the hotel meeting room with Kelly, my youngest daughter Sam and my son Sean, anxiously waiting for Robert to come into the room, I felt nervous. It was like being a young man again trying so hard to show that he had done a good job on something.

Something, as in your entire life.

I suppose this is like a son trying to prove himself to his father in some ways. Just more intense, even compared to how I was brought up by my dad. With my father, getting praise was like climbing to the mountain top. It was tough and painstaking, and it took weeks, if not months and years, to get there.

With the Fields family, this was something very different. Robert and Paula Fields had given me this precious gift in the wake of their tragic loss and here I was about to show them what I had done with it. You want them to know that something great had come from their painful experience, that their James' life hadn't been wasted by someone who didn't appreciate every moment, who didn't try to get everything he possibly could out of himself.

Counselors who specialize in this area of grief talk about how meetings can be incredibly emotional, potentially rekindling the most painful and difficult memories of that time.

For the briefest moment, that was true for Robert.

Before Robert walked in the hotel meeting room to meet my family, he smiled lightly, then walked in to meet the family he helped create through the loss of his son. A few steps later, Robert stopped as he saw us. For a moment, all his British sensibilities about decorum and understatement were gone.

He cried.

It was ever so brief and, in true British style, he apologized for it.

"You have James' heart and it's incredible," Robert said, looking at me and my family. "One of the nice things … is when I read that you had been a success. I said to myself, 'Isn't that great.' To see that the heart has gone somewhere and that someone has made use of it well. You haven't been that person that just sits in front of the television all day long."

I go over that moment again and again. The depth of Robert's emotional generosity was an amazing and touching thing to me. It made me feel so at ease. I just imagine in my head the tremendous courage Robert had to face that emotional moment and, in the face of it, make it so positive. Any way you look at it, you're meeting someone who has your son's heart and I could easily imagine feeling conflicted about it. I don't know if the tears created by all those emotions coming to a head at once, but Robert never showed even the slightest feeling of resentment and I am so extremely thankful for that.

Standing 6-foot-3 and with his full head of grey and white hair, Robert had a warm, gentle and humorous personality. I could see him as the perfect grandfather. He didn't take things too seriously, yet at the same time he understood the gravity of the moment. For those hours we spent together, he let me and my family in on his life and made me feel completely at ease.

This was the perfect ending to my search. For the better part of the past 25 years, I hadn't been that interested in pursuing a reunion. I'm not the most reflective person. That's part of my straightforward approach to life. I have always spent my life looking forward, not in retrospect. Since my transplant, I wasn't as concerned about who I received my heart from or what it meant because I had so much to do. But as this moment came closer and closer, I got more and more excited and intrigued.

Finding the Fields family didn't take a lot of work once I decided to do it myself. I started off going through Papworth Hospital, where I had the transplant surgery so many years ago. However, email after email went unanswered. I got some bureaucratic replies, but no answers and no progress. I understand it's part of the policy so that they can be respectful of the donor families. Still, it was frustrating.

That meant I had to take matters into my own hands. I had some newspaper articles from back then. One of the newspapers in England had run accompanying stories about James dying and me receiving a heart transplant. Because of the privacy laws, the newspaper couldn't get direct confirmation that I had received James' heart. In one article, there was mention of both me and James in the same story. It wasn't difficult to figure out.

I'm fortunate that the articles even exist. In 1986, the Fields family was very upset that the newspaper had put the articles together. Robert had gone so far as to call and complain to the editor about stirring up their family's grief. At another time, the newspaper might have thought twice about running the articles that way.

The article about James' death, along with an obituary that ran later, included enough information about the Fields family. From there, there was a lot of communication via phone calls and emails. I did my best to give them space and let them make the decision to talk to me, even though I was getting anxious to do this. I was hoping to get this reunion (that's an awkward way of putting it, but it works) to coincide with a family trip we were planning for Europe to celebrate Sam's high school graduation. Sean was going to Ireland to play in the famous Northern Ireland Milk Cup and the rest of us were going to meet him in London when he was done before heading to Italy.

Eventually, it all came together. Paula decided not to come. I so wish she had. She did try to call me that day, but she accidentally left the phone off the receiver at one point and the line was busy when I tried to call several times. At one point, we drove through the neighborhood and past the Fields' family home. Even though we had traveled more than 5,000 miles and I had waited more than 25 years to tell her thank you, I never for one second thought of intruding. This was an incredibly emotional day for everyone and I had to respect how Paula felt.

The other people I had to give some space to in the process were my family members, particularly Kelly. My wife has obviously been through a lot with me over the years. Just imagine the idea of marrying someone who had a heart transplant with a then-life expectancy of less than seven years. Then take the chance of starting and raising a family. I'm sure there are some people who think that would be a crazy idea if you look at it from a distance. But Kelly has grown used to life with me, mostly getting used to dealing with the fear.

Kelly has an incredible ability to manage me when it comes to my health. She's never heavy-handed or motherly. She's incredibly respectful and subtle. It has gotten to the point where Kelly will say something as simple as "maybe you should sleep in tomorrow." I'm a notorious early riser and sometimes I simply work myself into the ground without recognizing it. Or she will bring me two or three large glasses of water in a 20-minute span without me realizing because I may be on the verge of getting dehydrated. I am sure she has had fears. Between all the pacemaker replacements and an average of one surgery a year, she has seen it all.

Now, I was about to take her back over all of that and I'm sure it was uncomfortable. Actually, I know it was. It came right down to the day before the meeting before she made her decision to go with me. I completely understood.

I think my kids were a little more adventurous about the idea, particularly Sean. He said he wasn't going to miss this. The curiosity alone was enough to get him to come along. Sam was a little more on the fence about it, but probably closer to Sean in terms of wanting to be there. Our oldest daughter

Sarah stayed in Los Angeles and met us afterward. Kelly had her moments where you could see she was uncomfortable with this. But, as she always does, she pushed aside her apprehension and supported me completely and I felt that.

As for me, the anticipation was like nothing I'd gone through. For most things in my life, including big games, I never experienced this. In soccer, you practice and practice and practice. You know what you're supposed to do and you do it. Business is the same thing. Sure, things come up that you don't anticipate and you adjust. But you even know what the adjustments are going to be in most cases and can just react.

On the day before the meeting with Robert, as my family and I had driven from Eastbourne, where we had stayed with my cousin Nick his wife Karen and kids, I got increasingly giddy. Nervous, excited and even a little confused. Really, I can't remember feeling anything like this, it was such a weird state for me.

Again, I felt like I had something to prove, but not in a negative way or as if I had a chip on my shoulder, Rather, I wanted to make Robert happy that he had done this, that he and Paula had done something so great for me and that I didn't waste it. I wanted to say thank you, but how do you begin to say thank you for 25 years (and counting) of living? How do you say thank you for the joy of finding the perfect woman and having children with her? How do you say thank you for my beautiful daughters and wonderful son?

To be fair, I've met literally tens of thousands of organ recipients and putting all ego aside there is no doubt that I am one of, if not the most successful one ever. It does depend on how you define success. I have always defined it by the words Dr. Hakim uttered to me immediately post-surgery. "The goal of organ transplantation is to return to the life you were living prior to being sick." That was always my measuring stick. No other standard ever entered my mind. Of course, all success is contributed to a number of factors. It isn't because of me by myself. It wasn't because I could magically transform any heart and make it work. It's because James and I were a perfect fit. I don't say that lightly because it means our antigens were perfect, our blood type was perfect, and our size was perfect. Perhaps most importantly, we were connected in other, less scientific ways. Ways that are defy logical, easy explanation.

I don't have the words to express the depth of my gratitude. I'm not a man of many words when it relates to expressing my feelings and emotions. Within the confines of my simple, straightforward approach to life, I'm not terribly good at platitudes. Just like my father, praise doesn't flow out of me like an open spigot. But at this moment, I was ready to burst with whatever words came to the top of my head.

I also know how many other transplant recipients feel the same way. I talk about this moment when I speak to recipients and doctors at transplant conferences. It is, for most people, a tear-jerking moment. This has been a big change for me because I used to be so callous about this. When I first started speaking years ago, I didn't realize just how distant I was in respecting the contributions of the donors. I learned that after I did a talk one time in the United States in front of a large group of organ procurement organizations (or OPOs, as they are known).

When I was done speaking, my team handed out surveys and the overwhelming feedback I got from the people there was, "You're not paying enough respect to the donor." Not that I was treading on the donor or being disrespectful, but I was not giving them their due. What I needed to do was understand the sacrifice that people had made. Not so much the physical sacrifice, but the emotional one. This is not an easy thing for people to do, give up parts of their loved one or even for the individual to actively decide ahead of time to donate if they die. That's a level of generosity and forethought that I needed to be more cognizant of. It's part of what got me to think about the family that helped me and what I could do to pay proper respect. I'm sure that along the way, I've probably said things that made people think I wasn't at all respectful of the donors. It wasn't for lack of respect. It was more about me keeping focus on going forward.

So many people in my shoes never get that chance to meet the donor family, to express their gratitude. But as is my way, I had set a goal and I was focused to meet it.

So here I was. A moment I had pushed aside for more than a quarter of a century. We met in a hotel on a golf course just outside the city where James had lived up until he died. It was a warm August day. Robert came up to the room, entered and after those initial tears, the meeting couldn't have been more perfect.

Robert's initial reaction allayed my fears about how he would feel. Within minutes, he sounded more like a proud grandfather than someone who had suffered such a great loss 25 years ago.

"That, in a sense, is why one uses the word 'delight or pleasure' – all those very strong emotive words," Robert said. "Because yeah, it's going from one end of the spectrum to the other. Back then, about a year after the surgery, we received a letter about the donation with some information about how many people had received organs from James and how those people were doing. There weren't any names. They're merely telling you where the organs have gone. It was very impersonal, but that was the nature of how the system works."

For Robert, meeting us was a chance to see the results in person.

"It's great that some good is coming out of what was a tragic and sad situation. If you can help somebody, great," he said.

I explained to Robert how for years I had put all the thoughts and emotions about my transplant in a closet because it was counterproductive for me in where I was going. I just wanted to keep going forward and not really look back. I put myself in this little box of a world and lived right there. I talked about the speeches I had given, the feedback I had received and how much that caused me to want to finally have this reunion. I said to myself, I really have to do this. I've got to go say thank you. I knew there was nothing I could say to Robert to make him feel better about the loss of his son.

At one point Robert explained that although his family's loss was immeasurably painful, it was his son who lost the most. James had lost his future, his potential and all the possibilities that went with that. As Robert said those words, I heard one thing.

I had gained the most.

James had lost the most and I had gained the most.

From a boy I never knew and had no connection to, I had a received a gift I desperately needed. It's not guilt about that, because you can't live with guilt and I immediately got the feeling that Robert didn't want me to feel guilty. But it is there. I talked at length for years about how "somebody" had to die for me to live. For the longest time, it was "somebody X" and not an actual person I could talk about. I know that sounds terrible in some sense, but now I was at a point where I really wanted to know. I wanted to, in my own way, be close to James, to have some sort of connection.

Robert completely understood. He even looked at my children, smiled and joked: "You realize he's getting old, he's getting like me. It's only when you get to my age that you start thinking about that." In some sense, Robert did the same thing in dealing with the loss of his son.

"I can empathize very, very strongly with that because one of the ways for me to be able to handle the grief was to say, 'Look, life goes on. You've got to go forward.' You cannot keep saying 'James would want this, James would want that.' You've got to go and get on with your life. You are obviously very sad that this has happened because you've lost something, and the greatest sadness is what he lost. It's out of that tragedy that I said earlier, 'You hope that someone has used it well.' That's why I'm so pleased: A, to be able to meet you, and; B, to see what, where that precious organ has ended and being fully used in such a positive and successful way.

"It is good for me and I'm sure, in one sense, it will help me bring more closure."

I apologized to Robert for even bringing this all up again after so long. He said there was no reason for my apology.

"Don't for a start (begin to apologize)," Robert said. "It is good. I think sometimes it depends on why (the memory is) reopened. If the reason for the reopening is a good one, then there's nothing wrong with it. Let's look at it as an extension of the English. I don't like to use the expression 'giving his heart.' That is absolutely what happened, (but) it makes it far more gracious and pompous almost. We were doing something that was natural, not something that was a decision from on high that you should owe us something for. I don't know what it was like to be in that recipient situation. This is what I'm learning now.

"I spoke to my former doctor. He very recently retired and he lives two doors away. The other morning we were talking and I raised the subject with him because I thought that the names of the donors were confidential. That's how we got talking. What he said is that the heart is really just a pump, a muscle. People sometimes overlay it with so many other things. It is a rather important muscle, obviously, but in many ways it's just another piece of equipment that we have. You shouldn't make more of it than it is."

All of those thoughts fit right in with the way I had thought about the transplant early in life. One out, one in. Sure, it was callous. It's only after years and years that you look at the enormity of what you were able to do that you consider how special the gift was. This was my time to reflect on that gift.

From there, Robert showed us pictures of James and his family. He shared the stories about what James was like as a young man. He talked about the day James died. We talked about all the coincidences in the story, such as the fact that Sean's middle name is Edward, a family name (Kelly's father is Edward) and the same middle name as James and Robert. The fact that my dad was a teacher and so was Paula. The soccer background, everything.

Robert, who was in his 70s when we met, had the attitude of a younger man. He talked about how he loved to do "physical things" like cricket, tennis, ski, windsurf, sailing and cycling. He talked about how much he had traveled in retirement and his sometimes "naughty" sense of humor, which is more mischievous that actually naughty (at least in the American sense of naughty).

We spent more than two hours in that first part of the meeting and then went to lunch. It was a spectacular day at the hotel as we sat outside and continued to talk. Robert was just so inviting. As a result, he then became the greatest tour guide you could imagine.

We drove from the hotel to the city to see the neighborhood where James and his family lived. After driving by the family home, we ended up at the park where James died. I immediately noticed that one side of the park was bordered by Vancouver Street. I'm not a religious person, but I have a healthy streak of superstition. That was too coincidental for me. We parked on the street and walked down a short hill to the field.

That's where Kelly and Sean stopped. Kelly just observed and Sean went over to this little playground off to the side. Sam and I walked the field, arm-in-arm, silently and solemnly. This walk was very serious for me. This was like so many fields I had played on as a kid, a pretty neighborhood spot that would be filled with kids back when I was young. In the middle of a weekday, there were only a handful of people around.

Two little kids were playing soccer on the field, passing the ball between one another, an eerie reminder of what had been passed to me from this field.

I could imagine what it was like for a bunch of teenage boys to be out playing one Sunday afternoon and then be mortified as one of their friends passed out and died in front of them. That's not the type of thing you forget easily.

As we went back toward the edge of the field, Sean was even a little spooked. "I'm not going on that field. No way," he said. I understood.

Kelly looked on, silently making sure the kids were OK. Robert didn't say much.

As we left, Sam picked a wild flower from the side of the hill.

That took us to our final stop: James' grave.

The cemetery where he is buried is just down the street from the field and adjoins the neighborhood where he grew up. It's close enough that Paula can take a short walk there to be close to her son these days. The cemetery, like the vast majority of those in England, is hundreds of years old and divided up by religion. James' grave was toward the back of the cemetery.

When we got there, Robert, Sam, Sean and I got out of the car. Kelly wouldn't get out. Her reason was that Paula hadn't given us permission to do this. At the same time, Paula didn't say no, either. Kelly just felt uncomfortable intruding on that perceived space. Kelly is a mother, so I understand.

The four of us went to pay our respects. Robert comes here a couple of times a year, at least, including Christmas and James' birthday.

As we stood there, taking it all in, Sam took the wild flower and placed it on the grave. Robert thanked her and within a few moments his tears started to flow again. He talked about how much he regretted giving James an imperfect body and then made fun of himself for being a "big softie" as he tried to regain his composure. To me, this was enough. I had put the man through too much at that point, and I escorted him to a little privacy. Sam, Sean and I had a brief moment together at the grave, arm-in-arm not saying anything. What can you say at a moment like that?

They eventually left me to a last few moments. As I stood and looked at James' grave I couldn't help but focus on the date: July 7, 1986. Despite my bravado and attempts over the years to treat my transplant date "as just another day," it was nevertheless burned into me. It's almost a part of my DNA. For the first time the finality of the situation took hold. Here lay the young man who died in order for me to live. And as I stood there with Robert and asked him when he came here, he answered one of those days was always July 7. I told him that I thought about him each July 7, too, but until now it wasn't with a real sense of who James was. Now, I had a sense of who had helped me and I had a chance to show him proper respect.

And so we end where we've begun.

I stand in silent conversation with James.

I keep saying again and again, "We're going to do this together. We're going to make people understand how much I appreciate what I've received, and just how thankful I am…"

ABOUT THE AUTHORS

SIMON KEITH

Simon Keith holds the distinction of being the first athlete in the world to play a professional sport after undergoing a heart transplant. Keith was just 21 when, in July of 1986, he received the heart of a 17 year old boy, who ironically died while playing soccer. Keith, a world class soccer player prior to the operation, was determined to return to "his normal" and after playing at the University of Nevada, Las Vegas (UNLV) for two seasons, Keith was drafted number 1 overall into the Major Indoor Soccer League just three years after his surgery.

Now one of the longest living organ transplant recipients in the world and most notable professional athletes of his time, Keith travels cross-country captivating audiences with his "moments of truth" speeches and daring people to live.

In 2011, he founded The Simon Keith Foundation, an organization dedicated to increasing organ donor awareness and educating transplant recipients. Keith uses proceeds from his speaking engagements to provide athletic training for other transplant recipients who choose to return to an active and healthy lifestyle.

In addition to Keith's philanthropic efforts, and professional soccer career, he is a successful entrepreneur in Las Vegas, Nevada. More at www.thesimonkeithfoundation.com.

Jason Cole

Jason Cole is an NFL reporter for Yahoo! Sports. He has covered the league since 1992 and is the author of two books, as well as a contributing writer on four others. His first book was *Giant* with wide receiver and Super Bowl hero Plaxico Burress. His second was *Ocho Cinco*, an irreverent look at life with wide receiver Chad Ochocinco.

Prior to working for Yahoo!, Cole covered the Miami Dolphins for 15 years for both *The Miami Herald* and the *Fort Lauderdale Sun-Sentinel.* His work has earned awards and honors from what's arguably the most prestigious group in sports journalism, the Associated Press Sports Editors (APSE). He has also earned numerous awards from the Pro Football Writers of America, a Green Eyeshade award and was honored by the Florida State Sportswriters Association.

Cole's work helped push Yahoo!'s sports coverage to a higher level of respect in the ranks of internet journalism. He and Charles Robinson combined to do extensive investigative work, exposing that former USC running back and Heisman Trophy winner Reggie Bush received approximately $300,000 in cash and other benefits during his final season in college in direct violation of NCAA rules. Cole and Robinson followed that with an expose that accused USC men's basketball coach Tim Floyd of providing cash to a man who delivered future NBA star O.J. Mayo to the Trojans program. The stories ultimately led to USC being stripped of the 2005 Bowl Championship Series national title in football, being placed on probation and having scholarship reductions for the school. Bush became the first Heisman Trophy winner to give up the award. In addition, Floyd resigned as USC's coach.

Cole and Robinson's work also led to the book *Tarnished Heisman* by Don Yaeger, a detailed look in to the Bush saga.

Cole, a graduate of Stanford University, does more than 700 radio and television appearances each year to talk about the NFL and his other work. He also teaches sports writing and investigative reporting at the University of Florida.

Don Yaeger

Award-Winning Keynote Speaker, Seven-time New York Times Best-Selling Author, long-time Associate Editor for Sports Illustrated and Business Leader. Don Yaeger has fashioned a career that spans more than two decades. As an author, his books have sold more than 2 million copies and have been translated into more than a dozen languages. As an accomplished speaker, he delivers nearly 100 presentations a year to audiences as diverse as Fortune 25 companies and Cancer Survivor Groups, where he shares the story of his personal battle with cancer. He is principally sought-out to discuss lessons on achieving greatness, learned from first-hand experiences with some of the greatest sports legends in the world. Throughout his writing career, Don has developed a reputation as one of America's most provocative journalists and has been invited as a guest to every major talk show – from Oprah to Nightline, from CNN to Good Morning America. More at www.donyaeger.com.

Thank You

When you undertake a project like this it is SIMPLY IMPOSSIBLE to thank all the people that one needs to thank. This is particularly true in my case as this story took on a life of its own way back in 1984, continuing through today.

For those of you who were influential in my life as a youngster growing up in my hometown of Victoria British Columbia, and by extension Vancouver and all of Canada - Thank you. To all my "new" friends in my adopted hometown of Las Vegas, and the United States - Thank you. And for those in places far and wide – Thank you.

…It truly takes a village…

Heart for the Game was funded in part by the innovative social fundraising platform KICKSTARTER.com. This book is a reality because of the gracious support of the following people.

A. Steele-Mortimer
Adam C. DiOrio
Adam and Jill, Kyleigh, Coleman and Keegan Keith
Albert Guida Jr.
Amanda Richardson
Amy Flint
Andrew Weaver
Anne Mason Hall

Bernadette Arias
Bill and Cheryl Merriman
Bob and Pat Mielbrecht
Brett and Kelly Phillips
Brian Mousley
Bruce Cafferky
Carey Cleaver
Carlos and Kimberly Caipa
Chris and Tiffany Tettamanti

Coby Holt
Colin Richards
Colleen Kelly-Garraway
Colleen S Carter
Daniel
Daniel Corsatea
Daniel D. Barber
Darryl Pearson
Dave Ravenhill
Debbie
Denise Korach
Denison Cabral
Doug Waldie
Downtown Las Vegas Soccer Club
Parent
Dr. Neil Wells
Eddie Henderson
Elizabeth Miller
Eric A. Ashley
Frank and Cheryl Kocvara
George and Linda McKenna
Gerry Merz
Greg Balelo
Harry Newton and family
Ian, Debbie, Bryant & Megan Klitsie
In Memory of Brady Caipa
- From the Tonetti Family
Jackie Adkins
Jane Schum
Janice Hertlein
Jason DiOrio
Jay and Brenda Gould
Jean (Trumble) Kerfers
Jeanie and Mel Hendra
Jeff and Becky Skoll
Jeff and Kathy Smith
Jennifer Clay
Jerry Koloskie
Jill Hawe
Jim and Teri Mckusick
Jimmy Tufano and Camme Tyla
Jo-Anne

Jodi Lang
Joe and Patricia Pursell Family
Joe DeMarco
Joe Koziol
Joe Richards
Joel D. Wisner
John and Kim Barrera
John and Laura Millen
John and Miriam Lancaster
John de Goede
John Hanna
John Hou
John Howe
John Ogden
Jordan Lancaster
Judd and Jocelyn Tettamanti
Karen Kelsall
Kate Seiler
Kathi
Keith Bandy
Kevin Hall
Lee Khuong
Lane and Susan Kay
Larry Dennis
Leilani Austria
Les and Irena Bryan
Linda Bertuzzi
Liquid Nutrition Group
Lisa Andrews
Lisa Johnson
Liz Charsley-Jory
Lorenzo Erlic
Mac McDermid & family
Margaret McCormick
Mark Buyens
Matt Engle
Matthew and Jamie Chilton
McAdams Family
Michael Mack
Michael O'Brien
Michael Ravenhill
Micka Sorani

Mike and the Skillings Family
Militello Family
Mitchell Cohen
Mr. & Mrs. Bert Mukkulainen
Ms. Jessica Legut
Murray Smith
Neil Ryan
Patricia Taylor
Patty Dundore
Paul and Lisa Chao
Paul Sparrow
Peter M Barrera
Pip Charsley
Rich and Vanes Ryerson
Richard and Hilary Glass
Ridge J Mahoney
Rob and Linda Taber
Robert J Eckels
Robert Speciale
Roberta Tettamanti
Roger and Amy Tabor
Roslyn and Dwayne Peleshaty
Ross and Kristin Smith
Ryan and Kelly May
Scott Longpre
Shannon Alvarez
Sharon
Shawn Shawl
Shawna Ballard, LLC.
Southern Nevada Sports Hall of Fame
Stacy Martello
Stephanie and Steve Stallworth
Stephen Dorsey
Steve, Kelly and Nathan Bohn
Sundog Eyewear
Tak and Kathy Niketas
Team Weinberg
Terri Cullen-Stewart
The Aitchison Family
The Borgel Family
The Goble Family, Eastbourne, UK
The Kopp family

The Marwood Family
The Mielbrecht Family
The Mosher Family
The OnlineSoccerAcademy.com
The Porrello Family
The Raptis Family
The Segler Family
The Wilson Family
Tim and Bridget Keener
Tim Dakin
Tina Anderson
Todd Udall
Tracy Jones
Walter A. Mroziak
Wayne and Robin Volesky
Wendy
Wendy Reese
William Coulthard
Yvonne Walsh

Many other people contributed greatly to the success of Heart for the Game. Here are just a few of those people.

Alex Robertson
Barry Barto
Brian Williams
Dale Eeles
Dick Calvert
Nevada Colwell
Paul Palmer
Rob Portaro
Scott Weinberg

A SPEAKER WHO DARES YOU TO LIVE

Speaker, Author, Professional Athlete, Successful Businessman…and oh yeah…Heart Transplant Recipient more than 25 years ago. Simon Keith holds the distinction of being the first athlete in the world to play a professional sport after undergoing a heart transplant. Keith was just 21 when, in July of 1986, he received the heart of a 17 year old boy, who ironically died while playing soccer. Keith, a world class soccer player prior to the operation, was determined to return to "his normal" and after playing at the University of Nevada, Las Vegas (UNLV) for two seasons, Keith was drafted number 1 overall into the Major Indoor Soccer League just three years after his surgery. Now one of the longest living organ transplant recipients in the world and most notable professional athletes of his time, Keith travels cross-country captivating audiences with his "moments of truth" speeches and daring people to live.
In 2011, he founded The Simon Keith Foundation, an organization dedicated to increasing organ donor awareness and educating transplant recipients. Keith uses the proceeds from his speaking engagements to provide athletic training for other transplant recipients who choose to return to an active and healthy lifestyle.

THE SIMON KEITH FOUNDATION

The Simon Keith Foundation is dedicated to providing financial support primarily to youths who have undergone a life-saving organ transplant who desire a return to an active and healthy lifestyle. In addition to helping people with their non-medical expenses, the Foundation strives to increase organ donor registration through public awareness campaigns.

Website: www.thesimonkeithfoundation.com

E-Mail: Simon@thesimonkeithfoundation.com

Facebook: www.facebook.com/thesimonkeithfoundation

Twitter: @simonkeith1

MOMENTS OF TRUTH

How Do You Identify?
How Do You Prepare?
And How Do You Maximize Your Moments Of Truth?

THE RECIPE TO BECOME A CHAMPION

PREPARE: Champions prepare more, and harder, than others

WHEN NO ONE IS LOOKING: Champions put in the work when no one is looking. And we mean real work.

MOTIVATION: Ultimately this comes from within. Champions have an endless supply of self-motivation

CHARACTER: Forget about reputation. Champions focus on character.

THE POWER OF STUPID: Champions ignore the negatives and turn off the part of the brain that says it can't be done

RELENTLESS PURSUIT OF EXCELLENCE: Champions are simply relentless in the pursuit of their goals

DARE TO LIVE: Champions love clichés. Just Do it! Make it Happen! Get on with it!

To learn more about how to book Simon to speak at your event log onto: www.thesimonkeithfoundation.com.

Made in the USA
San Bernardino, CA
05 April 2014